I0114072

THE STRATEGIC BLUEPRINT FOR MEDICAL PRACTICE

Maximizing Revenue and Streamlining Operations

Bernadette Albury, MHA

The Strategic Blueprint for Medical Practice
Maximizing Revenue and Streamlining Operations

Publisher
Bernadette Albury, MHA
Pembroke Pines, Florida

Cover Design by Priscilla Pope
Duluth, Georgia

Book Completion Services Provided by:
TRU Statement Publications—Independent Publishing Made Easy
www.trustatementpublications.com

Disclaimer
This book is intended for informational purposes only and does not provide medical, legal, or other professional advice. The author and publisher disclaim any liability arising directly or indirectly from the use of information contained in this book. Readers should consult with a professional in the relevant field before applying any of the information in this book to their own practice.

For permissions, requests, or inquiries, contact:
info@gatewayhealthcaresolutions.com

First Edition: April 2025
Printed in the United States of America

TABLE OF CONTENTS

THE STRATEGIC BLUEPRINT FOR MEDICAL PRACTICE

Maximizing Revenue and Streamlining Operations

HISTORY OF MEDICAL PRACTICE IN THE UNITED STATES

When did private practices for doctors begin in the United States?

The concept of physicians operating private practices is well established in the United States. While it is difficult to pinpoint the exact date of the first physician's private practice, several historical milestones contributed to the development of medical practices as we know them today.

Early 19th Century: By the early 1800s, medicine in the United States had become more formalized. Physicians established private practices in towns and cities, offering medical services to local residents. These practices were often the primary source of medical care for many Americans.

Medical Education: The founding of medical schools in the eighteenth and nineteenth centuries, such as the University of Pennsylvania's Perelman School of Medicine in 1765, helped standardize medical education and training. This standardization contributed to the professionalization of medicine and the growth of private medical practices.

Urbanization and Industrialization: As cities and industries expanded during the nineteenth century, demand for medical services grew. Many physicians moved from rural communities to urban centers, where they could open private practices and serve larger populations.

Regulation and Licensing: Over time, state and local governments began to regulate the practice of medicine by requiring licensure. These measures helped ensure that only qualified individuals could practice medicine, lending legitimacy to the profession and to private practices in particular.

A multitude of historical, social, and economic factors have shaped the complex and multifaceted history of private medical practices in the United States. Though the exact date of the first American physician's private practice is unknown, we can trace the origins of private medicine back to the colonial era.

During colonial times, independent medical practitioners frequently served their local communities by offering general medical care. These early clinics were typically modest, but they laid the foundation for the more structured practices that emerged in the following centuries.

In the early 1800s, the formal organization of medical practice gained momentum. The founding of institutions like the Perelman School of Medicine furthered the standardization of instruction and training. As medical knowledge advanced, physicians were increasingly able to create structured and professional private clinics.

Urbanization and industrialization throughout the nineteenth century dramatically influenced the growth of private practice. Physicians relocated to cities to meet the increasing demand for healthcare, and as governments introduced licensing regulations, the credibility and structure of medical practice improved.

Over time, private medical practices became a cornerstone of the American healthcare system. Today, they continue to provide essential medical services to communities across the country.

Key References

Books

- *The Social Transformation of American Medicine* by Paul Starr
- *American Medical Association: A History, 1847–1947* by Morris Fishbein

Articles

- "The Development of Medical Practice in the United States: 1900–1984" by John L. Field
- "Physicians' Practice Arrangements: 1956–1981" by James D. Reschovsky

Websites

- American Medical Association – History of Medicine: https://www.ama-assn.org/about/ama-history/history-medicine
- National Library of Medicine – History of Medicine Division: https://www.nlm.nih.gov/hmd/index.html

INTRODUCTION

The healthcare landscape is ever evolving, and the demands on physicians have become increasingly complex. As healthcare providers strive to deliver high-quality patient care while managing administrative tasks, there is a growing need for a comprehensive guide that empowers physicians with the knowledge and tools to optimize their practices efficiently.

This *How-to Guide for Physicians' Practice* is designed to equip medical professionals with essential strategies, best practices, and resources to enhance practice management, streamline workflows, and ultimately improve patient outcomes.

Purpose of the Guide

This guide aims to provide physicians with a structured approach to effectively managing their medical practices, prioritizing three main objectives:

1. **Practice Efficiency**

   Efficient practice management is paramount to maximizing time spent on patient care and reducing administrative burdens. This guide explores techniques and technologies that streamline scheduling, billing, documentation, and communication, fostering a more efficient and smooth-running practice.

2. **Enhancing Patient Care**

   At the core of every physician's mission is delivering high-quality patient care. This guide outlines methods for optimizing patient engagement, communication, and education, which strengthens the doctor-patient relationships and promoting better health outcomes.

3. **Navigating Regulatory and Legal Challenges**

   Physicians face an ever-changing landscape of regulations and legal complexities. This guide provides insights on navigating compliance issues, protecting patient data, and staying informed about current healthcare laws.

Overview of Components Covered in the Guide

Practice Management

□ *Setting Up a Successful Practice:* Key considerations for starting a medical practice, including choosing a location, defining the practice's mission and values, and creating a business plan.

□ *Staffing and Team Building:* Strategies for assembling a competent and cohesive team, delegating responsibilities, and fostering a positive work culture.

□ *Efficient Scheduling and Time Management:* Techniques for optimizing appointment scheduling, reducing patient wait times, and managing a physician's time effectively.

□ *Medical Billing and Coding:* A comprehensive overview of billing and coding practices to ensure accurate and timely reimbursement while adhering to coding guidelines.

□ *Electronic Health Records (EHR) Implementation:* Insights on selecting, adopting, and integrating EHR systems for improved patient care, data security, and documentation efficiency.

Patient Engagement and Communication

□ *Improving Doctor–Patient Communication:* Effective strategies for building trust, enhancing patient understanding, and promoting active patient participation.

□ *Empowering Patients with Health Education:* Tips for creating and sharing educational materials to promote health literacy and informed decision-making.

□ *Utilizing Telemedicine:* Leveraging telehealth technologies to expand access, monitor chronic conditions, and enhance convenience.

□ *Enhancing the Patient Experience:* Techniques to improve satisfaction within the practice, including waiting room management, appointment reminders, and feedback mechanisms.

Regulatory Compliance and Risk Management

□ *Staying Compliant with Healthcare Regulations:* An overview of significant regulations such as HIPAA, Medicare/Medicaid rules, and the Affordable Care Act, with practical steps for compliance.

□ *Data Privacy and Security:* Best practices for protecting patient information, securing electronic records, and mitigating risks of data breaches.

□ *Medical Malpractice Prevention:* Strategies to reduce malpractice risk and enhance patient safety.

Financial Management

□ *Budgeting and Financial Planning:* Guidance on developing a financial plan, managing cash flow, and making informed financial decisions to support sustainability.

□ *Optimizing Revenue Cycle Management:* Strategies to enhance revenue collection, reduce claim denials, and minimize accounts receivable.

Balancing Work–Life Integration

□ *Physician Well-being:* Prioritizing self-care, managing stress, and preventing burnout to support professional longevity.

□ *Work–Life Balance Strategies:* Techniques to maintain a thriving practice while nurturing a healthy personal life.

WHY YOU NEED A CLINICAL STAFF ONBOARDING GUIDE

An effective onboarding plan for physicians and clinical staff is not optional—it is essential. While some practices may focus primarily on medical expertise, overlooking administrative onboarding and business processes can be a costly oversight. A well-structured onboarding process benefits everyone involved, from the provider to the staff to the patients.

The same principle applies to other aspects of provider onboarding. Best practices include creating online portals that allow new physicians to submit required documentation prior to their first day. In the Physician Onboarding Plan that follows (which can also be adapted for physician assistants [PAs] and nurse practitioners [NPs]), many elements can be uploaded to an online platform. This leaves both providers and staff free to focus on the practical aspects of integrating new clinicians into the practice.

Benefits of a Successful Onboarding Process

Retention: Investing time in a thoughtful and seamless onboarding experience signals to staff that their comfort and success matter. This establishes loyalty and improves staff retention, ultimately saving the practice money by reducing turnover.

Efficiency: Organizations of all sizes benefit from a standardized and consistent workflow. When every team member follows the same procedures as outlined in the healthcare onboarding plan, new hires learn daily processes more quickly and with fewer errors.

Collaboration: Early relationship-building among staff during onboarding helps establish trust. When all team members receive the same training and understand how to work together effectively, collaboration is stronger and more reliable.

Morale: Medical practice is a dynamic field, with continuous opportunities for learning. A culture that prioritizes training, mentorship, and cooperation boosts job satisfaction and supports long-term career development.

Patient Satisfaction: Patients notice when clinical staff are confident, cooperative, and valued. When team morale is high and workflows are aligned, patient experiences improve, which leads to a higher satisfaction and trust in the practice.

CHAPTER 1
PATIENT DEMOGRAPHICS

Patient demographics play a vital role in healthcare, providing essential insights into the characteristics and backgrounds of individuals seeking medical services. This information helps healthcare providers better understand their patient population and tailor care accordingly. Key demographic details typically include age, gender, ethnicity, marital status, language, education level, employment status, income, geographic location, insurance coverage, medical history, and social history.

By analyzing patient demographics, healthcare professionals can identify patterns in health conditions that may be more prevalent within specific groups. This knowledge enables targeted preventive care and early interventions to address potential health disparities. For example, certain diseases may be more common in specific age groups or ethnicities, and providers can use that information to implement appropriate screenings and patient education.

Importance of Accurate Patient Demographic Information

Accurate demographic data is critical in healthcare for several reasons:

Personalized and Effective Care: Understanding accurate demographic information allows healthcare providers to deliver personalized care. Each demographic group, whether defined by age, gender, ethnicity, or socioeconomic status, may have distinct healthcare needs. By recognizing these factors, healthcare professionals can tailor treatment plans and interventions to improve outcomes for each individual.

Patient Safety and Identification: Correct demographic data ensures accurate patient identification. Verifying names, birthdates, and other identifying information helps prevent medical errors and supports accurate recordkeeping.

Continuity of Care: Precise demographic information contributes to the continuity of care. When patients move or change providers, complete and accurate demographic data ensures seamless transfer of records, reducing duplication and care gaps.

Health Records and Data Management: Demographic data forms a foundational component of electronic health records (EHRs). Effective data management enables timely access to patient records and supports well-informed clinical decisions. It also improves medical research and public health studies by providing reliable data for analysis and reporting.

Access to Care and Resources: Accurate demographic information helps identify healthcare disparities and ensures equitable access to resources. Policymakers and healthcare organizations can use this data to allocate services more effectively and reach underserved populations.

Regulatory Compliance: Healthcare organizations must comply with regulations such as the Health Insurance Portability and Accountability Act (HIPAA). Accurate demographic records are essential for ensuring compliance, protecting patient privacy, and maintaining confidentiality.

Health Insurance and Billing: Correct demographic information supports accurate billing and reimbursement. It helps confirm insurance coverage, verify identities, and reduce errors in claims processing.

Public Health and Epidemiology: Accurate patient demographic data is vital for public health tracking and epidemiological research. It supports the identification of risk factors and enables the design of targeted interventions for specific communities.

Collecting and Verifying Patient Information During Registration

When registering patients, healthcare providers must collect and verify critical demographic data to ensure accurate and effective care delivery. Below is a breakdown of essential information to gather:

Personal Information

- **Full Name:** The patient's legal name, including first, middle (if applicable), and last names, to ensure proper identification.
- **Date of Birth:** Used to verify age and eligibility for age-specific services.
- **Gender:** Important for determining gender-related healthcare needs.
- **Marital Status:** May affect medical decision-making and support systems.

- **Language Preference:** Helps ensure effective communication and allows the practice to offer interpreter services, if needed.

Contact Information

- **Address:** Full residential address, including street, city, state, postal code, and country.
- **Phone Number:** Primary contact number(s) for scheduling and follow-up.
- **Email Address:** (If available) Used for electronic communication, updates, and reminders.

Insurance and Financial Information

- **Insurance Provider:** To ensure proper billing and coverage.
- **Policy Number:** Unique identifier tied to the patient's insurance.
- **Group Number:** If applicable, linked to the employer or organization providing the policy.
- **Policyholder's Name:** If different from the patient (e.g., spouse, parent).
- **Co-payment/Co-insurance:** Out-of-pocket costs for each visit or service.
- **Deductibles:** Amount the patient must pay before insurance coverage begins.
- **Authorizations and Referrals:** If required for specialist visits or services.

Medical History and Health Information

- **Medical Conditions:** Chronic illnesses, previous diagnoses, and other relevant history.
- **Allergies:** Known allergies to medications, foods, or environmental triggers.
- **Medications:** All current prescriptions, over-the-counter drugs, supplements, and vitamins.
- **Family Medical History:** Information on hereditary conditions or genetic risks.

Emergency Contact Information

- **Emergency Contact Name:** Person to notify in case of emergency.
- **Relationship to Patient:** (e.g., spouse, parent, sibling).
- **Emergency Contact Number:** Reliable phone number for urgent communication.

Best Practices for Maintaining Patient Records Securely and Efficiently

Maintaining secure and efficient patient records is essential for protecting privacy, ensuring compliance, and enabling high-quality care. The following best practices help safeguard patient data:

Implement an Electronic Health Records (EHR) System: Use a secure, HIPAA-compliant EHR system to digitize and centralize patient data. Ensure encryption and access controls are in place to protect information.

Access Controls and User Authentication: Restrict access to authorized personnel only. Use multi-factor authentication for all user logins to prevent unauthorized access.

Regular Staff Training: Conduct ongoing training for staff on handling confidential data. Emphasize privacy, HIPAA requirements, and proper data entry protocols.

Data Backup and Recovery: Routinely back up records to secure, offsite servers. Implement a disaster recovery plan to restore data in case of emergencies or cyberattacks.

Audit Reporting and Monitoring: Track system access and monitor for unusual or unauthorized activity. Maintain logs of who accesses which records and when.

Regular Software Updates and Security Patches: Keep all systems current with updates and patches to protect against known vulnerabilities.

Securing Physical Records (if applicable): Store physical files in locked cabinets with limited access. Maintain a check-out system to track movement of any paper documents.

Secure Communication: Use encrypted email or secure messaging for sensitive communications. Avoid discussing confidential patient details in public or over unsecured lines.

Data Encryption: Encrypt all patient data in transit and at rest to protect against breaches.

Establish a Privacy Policy: Create and maintain a written policy that outlines how patient data is collected, stored, shared, and protected. Obtain patient consent and educate them about their rights under HIPAA.

Chapter Reflection and Implementation Notes

What New Insights Did I Gain?

(Use this space to reflect on key takeaways from this chapter.)

How Can I Apply These Principles in My Practice?

(Note actionable steps or ideas inspired by this chapter.)

Additional Notes

(Use the lines below for any further notes, ideas, or observations.)

CHAPTER 2
INSURANCE VERIFICATION

Insurance verification is a critical process in the healthcare industry that involves confirming a patient's insurance coverage and benefits before providing medical services. This foundational step ensures accurate billing, timely reimbursement, and a seamless patient experience, which are three essential components of a financially sustainable and patient-centered medical practice.

In today's complex healthcare environment, providers must navigate a wide range of insurance policies, coverage limitations, and payer-specific requirements. Without a consistent and thorough verification process, even the most skilled clinical team can face financial setbacks due to denied claims, delayed payments, or unexpected patient balances.

Accurate insurance verification also plays a key role in transparency and trust. It allows practices to clearly communicate financial responsibilities to patients before services are rendered, preventing billing disputes and improving satisfaction. As healthcare costs continue to rise, and patients become more involved in their own financial planning, this proactive approach is no longer optional—it's expected.

This chapter outlines the essential steps, tools, and best practices needed to implement an effective insurance verification system and highlights common pitfalls to avoid. When done correctly, insurance verification not only protects the financial health of the practice but also reinforces a smooth, respectful, and informed patient experience.

Purpose of Insurance Verification

Insurance verification serves several essential purposes:

- **Accurate Billing:** Ensures that claims are submitted to the correct insurance company, reducing denials due to incorrect or outdated information.
- **Eligibility Confirmation:** Verifies that the patient's insurance policy is active and that they are eligible for requested services.
- **Coverage and Benefits:** Provides information on co-pays, deductibles, and coverage limitations, enabling providers to inform patients of their financial responsibilities.
- **Preauthorization Requirements:** Identifies services requiring prior approval, reducing claim denials.
- **Patient Communication:** Equips providers to explain financial obligations clearly, improving transparency and trust.

Process of Insurance Verification

A typical insurance verification process involves the following steps:

- **Gathering Information:** Collect the patient's insurance card and personal details such as full name, date of birth, and policy number.
- **Contacting the Insurance Company:** Reach out to the insurer via phone or a secure online portal to verify coverage and benefits.
- **Verifying Patient Information:** Provide necessary patient details to authenticate the request.

- **Verifying Coverage and Benefits:** Confirm the policy status, covered services, co-pays, and deductibles.
- **Documenting Results:** Record all verification details in the patient's electronic health record (EHR) or practice management system.

Significance of Insurance Verification

Insurance verification is essential for the following reasons:

- **Financial Stability:** Supports timely and accurate reimbursement.
- **Improved Patient Experience:** Informs patients of their financial responsibilities in advance.
- **Reduced Claim Denials:** Minimizes errors and eligibility-related denials.
- **Compliance and Transparency:** Promotes alignment with insurance requirements and ethical billing.
- **Efficient Workflow:** Ensures smooth administrative processes and reduces billing-related disruptions during appointments.

Importance of Insurance Verification for Billing and Claims Processing

A robust insurance verification process is foundational for accurate billing and efficient claims management. Its benefits include:

Accurate Billing

- **Verification of Coverage:** Confirms that the insurance policy is current.
- **Correct Information:** Prevents errors by validating policy numbers and company data.
- **Coverage and Benefits:** Helps estimate patient financial responsibility based on verified insurance benefits.

Timely Reimbursement

- **Preauthorization:** Identifies services requiring prior approval to avoid delays.
- **Eligibility Confirmation:** Ensures coverage for services provided.
- **Reduced Denials:** Limits rejections due to eligibility or coverage errors.

Streamlined Claims Processing

- **Fewer Disputes:** Reduces billing confusion by managing patient expectations.
- **Efficient Workflow:** Enhances claim submission speed and accuracy.

- **Focus on Care:** Allows staff to prioritize patient care over administrative issues.

Enhanced Patient Satisfaction

- **Transparency in Billing:** Builds trust through upfront communication.
- **Reduced Financial Stress:** Provides clarity about coverage and out-of-pocket costs.

Compliance and Documentation

- **Insurance Requirements:** Ensures adherence to payer rules.
- **Accurate Documentation:** Supports audits and internal reviews.

Financial Stability

- **Timely Payments:** Improves cash flow with fewer claim errors.
- **Reduced Revenue Loss:** Prevents underpayments and denied claims.

Step-by-Step Instructions for Verifying Patient Insurance Coverage

Follow these steps to conduct a thorough insurance verification:

1. **Gather Patient Information**
    - Obtain a current insurance card.
    - Confirm the patient's full name, date of birth, and contact information.
2. **Contact the Insurance Company**
    - Call the insurer using the number on the card or access the online portal.
3. **Authenticate the Request**
    - Provide necessary credentials and patient data to initiate the verification.
4. **Verify Policy Details**
    - Confirm the policy number and ensure it matches the patient's information.
    - Check that the policy is active.
5. **Check Eligibility and Coverage**
    - Verify service eligibility.
    - Determine co-pays, deductibles, and any exclusions.
6. **Identify Preauthorization Requirements**
    - Check whether prior approval is needed.

- Obtain authorization as required.

7. **Document the Results**
    - Record the verification details in the EHR or management system.
    - Include notes on coverage and limitations.
8. **Inform the Patient**
    - Explain insurance details and out-of-pocket costs.
9. **Update Billing Information**
    - Enter the correct insurance data into the billing system.
10. **Follow Up if Necessary**
    - Resolve outstanding issues with the insurer.
    - Keep the patient updated on changes.
11. **Maintain HIPAA Compliance**
    - Protect patient information and follow privacy laws throughout the process.
12. **Document the Process**
    - Track steps taken for internal auditing and compliance purposes.

Common Issues in Insurance Verification and How to Address Them

Issue	Solution
Outdated Insurance Information	Require patients to verify and update insurance at each visit.
Delayed Insurance Responses	Begin verification well before appointments; use online portals when possible.
Lack of Preauthorization	Train staff on services that require preauthorization; establish tracking systems.
Incomplete or Inaccurate Information	Double-check all patient data; train staff on thorough intake procedures.
Eligibility Changes	Re-verify eligibility before each visit; update records regularly.
Communication Challenges	Use clear, secure communication methods with insurers; document thoroughly.
Complex Insurance Plans	Educate staff on plan variations; develop reference tools for common providers.
Denied Claims	Analyze rejections and appeal with supporting documentation when necessary.
Limited Insurance Knowledge	Provide ongoing training on insurance verification and payer requirements.
Privacy and Security Concerns	Follow HIPAA guidelines; use secure systems and limit access to sensitive data.
Lack of Follow-Up	Implement systems to track pending verifications and ensure timely resolution.

Unclear Coverage Terminology	Train staff to interpret insurance jargon; maintain a glossary of common terms.
Frequent Policy Changes	Encourage patients to notify the practice of job or plan changes immediately; verify coverage at every encounter.
High Deductible Plans	Educate staff to explain deductibles clearly to patients; collect pre-service estimates when possible.
Coordination of Benefits (COB) Delays	Identify when a patient has dual coverage; verify which plan is primary before billing.
Out-of-Network Services	Confirm network participation before scheduling; inform patients of additional costs when out-of-network.
Manual Verification Bottlenecks	Invest in real-time verification software and tools integrated with your EHR system.
Authorization Not Communicated to Front Desk	Establish workflows to ensure prior authorizations are clearly documented and visible to scheduling and front desk teams.
Missing Secondary Insurance	Ask during intake if patients have secondary insurance; record and verify all coverage.
Coverage Terminated Retroactively	Periodically confirm coverage status post-visit for high-risk payers; ask patients to verify before follow-up appointments.

Chapter Reflection and Implementation Notes

What New Insights Did I Gain?

(Use this space to reflect on key takeaways from this chapter.)

How Can I Apply These Principles in My Practice?

(Note actionable steps or ideas inspired by this chapter.)

Additional Notes

(Use the lines below for any further notes, ideas, or observations.)

CHAPTER 3
BILLING SHEET TEMPLATE

A billing sheet is a fundamental tool in healthcare practices, used to document patient services and their corresponding charges. A well-designed billing sheet ensures accuracy in charge capture, streamlines administrative workflows, and supports efficient claims processing.

Beyond its administrative role, the billing sheet serves as a bridge between clinical care and financial operations. It helps translate the services rendered into standardized codes and charges that comply with insurance requirements and legal regulations. Inaccurate or incomplete billing documentation can lead to claim denials, revenue loss, and compliance risks, making it vital for practices to maintain a consistent and detailed billing process.

Moreover, a structured billing sheet supports internal accountability and transparency. It enables billing staff, clinical teams, and auditors to track each service provided, ensuring that all billable procedures are accurately recorded and properly reimbursed. In today's healthcare landscape, where providers face increasing pressure to maintain both clinical excellence and operational efficiency, a reliable billing template is not just helpful; it is essential.

The following section introduces a customizable billing sheet template and offers practical guidance on how to use each part effectively.

Below is a basic billing sheet template that can be customized to suit the needs of your practice or healthcare organization.

BILLING SHEET TEMPLATE

[Your Healthcare Practice/Organization Name] Billing Sheet

Date: [Date of Service]

Patient Name: [Patient's Full Name]

Patient ID: [Patient's Unique Identifier]

Service Date	CPT Code	Descrip-tion	Units	Unit Price	Total Charges
[MM/DD/YY]	[CPT Code]	[Service Description]	[Units]	[$ Unit Price]	[$ Total]
[MM/DD/YY]	[CPT Code]	[Service Description]	[Units]	[$ Unit Price]	[$ Total]
[MM/DD/YY]	[CPT Code]	[Service Description]	[Units]	[$ Unit Price]	[$ Total]

- **Subtotal:** [Total Charges Before Any Additional Fees]
- **Total Amount Due:** [Final Patient Responsibility]

Payment Details

- **Payment Method:** [Cash / Credit Card / Insurance / Other]
- **Payment Date:** [Date of Payment]
- **Amount Paid:** [Amount Paid]
- **Notes:** [Add relevant notes or special instructions]

Thank you for choosing [Your Healthcare Practice/Organization Name].

For billing inquiries, please contact us at [Contact Information].

Introducing a Standardized Billing Sheet

Using a standardized billing sheet supports a consistent, clear, and error-free billing process. It benefits both the provider and the patient by improving accuracy, communication, and reimbursement timelines.

Guidelines for Using the Billing Sheet

- **Date of Service:** Record the date services were rendered.
- **Patient Information:** Include full name and a unique patient ID.
- **Service Details:** Document the service date, CPT code, service description, number of units, unit price, and total charges.
- **Subtotal:** Calculate the subtotal before additional fees.
- **Total Amount Due:** Add any additional fees to determine the final balance.
- **Payment Details:** Note the payment method, date, and amount paid.
- **Notes:** Record any special billing notes or instructions.
- **Contact Information:** Provide billing contact details for patient inquiries.

Section Breakdown and Purpose

Each section of the billing sheet plays a vital role in ensuring complete and accurate billing documentation:

- **Date of Service:** Tracks when each medical service was provided, aiding chronological recordkeeping.
- **Patient Name and Patient ID:** Ensures the bill is linked to the correct patient and reduces the risk of identification errors.
- **CPT Code and Description:** The Current Procedural Terminology (CPT) code specifies the service provided, while the description explains the procedure in plain terms for clarity.
- **Units and Unit Price:** Shows how many of each service were provided and the cost per unit. Total Charges are calculated by multiplying Units × Unit Price.
- **Total Charges and Subtotal:** Offers transparency by showing the cost of individual services and the subtotal before extra fees.
- **Total Amount Due:** Represents the full balance owed by the patient, including all services and applicable charges.
- **Payment Details:** Records the type and amount of payment received and the transaction date.
- **Notes:** Offers space for special instructions, clarifications, payment plans, or unique billing arrangements.
- **Contact Information:** Helps patients seek support with billing questions, improving communication and satisfaction.

Tips for Error-Free Data Entry

Accurate data entry is essential for financial integrity and compliance in healthcare operations. Consider the following best practices:

- **Double-Check Entries:** Review all data before moving on to the next field.
- **Use Validation Rules:** Establish automated checks for dates, codes, and formats to prevent invalid entries.
- **Restrict Data Access:** Limit data entry privileges to trained personnel only.
- **Standardize Formats:** Use consistent formats for dates, phone numbers, addresses, and names.
- **Provide Staff Training:** Ensure all users are trained on the billing system and procedures.
- **Avoid Multitasking:** Encourage staff to focus on one task at a time to minimize mistakes.
- **Use Drop-Down Menus:** Implement pre-set options for fields like CPT codes or insurance types.
- **Monitor Error Reports:** Review system reports to identify and address recurring mistakes.
- **Implement Error Correction Protocols:** Establish a formal process to log, correct, and track data errors.
- **Conduct Regular Audits:** Periodically review billing entries to ensure accuracy and uncover patterns.
- **Provide Clear Instructions:** Define complex fields, abbreviations, and exceptions in a reference guide.

- **Automate Where Possible:** Automate repetitive or high-volume data entry fields when appropriate.
- **Backup Data Regularly:** Prevent data loss by implementing daily or weekly backups.
- **Seek Staff Feedback:** Encourage front-line users to recommend improvements to the data entry process.

Notes

Example Billing Sheet Table

Here is a sample of a completed billing sheet:

[Your Healthcare Practice/Organization Name] – Billing Sheet

- **Date:** 10/01/2024
- **Patient Name:** Jane Smith
- **Patient ID:** 123456789

Service Date	CPT Code	Description	Units	Unit Price	Total Charges
10/01/24	99213	Office Visit - Level 3	1	$150.00	$150.00
10/01/24	87070	Urine Culture	1	$75.00	$75.00
10/01/24	80053	Comprehensive Metabolic Panel	1	$200.00	$200.00

Subtotal: $425.00

Total Amount Due: $425.00

Payment Details:

Payment Method: Insurance
Payment Date: 10/05/2024
Amount Paid: $425.00

Notes: [Add any relevant notes or special instructions here]

Thank you for choosing [Your Healthcare Practice/Organization Name]. For any billing inquiries, please contact us at [Contact Information].

Chapter Reflection and Implementation Notes

What New Insights Did I Gain?

(Use this space to reflect on key takeaways from this chapter.)

How Can I Apply These Principles in My Practice?

(Note actionable steps or ideas inspired by this chapter.)

Additional Notes

(Use the lines below for any further notes, ideas, or observations.)

CHAPTER 4
CREDENTIALING REQUIREMENTS

Credentialing is a foundational process in modern healthcare operations. It involves gathering, verifying, and evaluating a provider's professional qualifications, including education, licensure, certifications, work history, and legal standing. Proper credentialing ensures that medical professionals meet the established standards of safety, competence, and regulatory compliance required by insurers and governing bodies.

Whether for individual practitioners or group practices, the credentialing process is critical for participating in insurance networks, maintaining trust with patients, and receiving timely reimbursement for services rendered. Credentialing also plays a key role in upholding public health standards by ensuring that only qualified providers are permitted to deliver care under payer contracts.

This chapter outlines the core components of credentialing, including required documents, submission timelines, the use of platforms like CAQH, and the practical steps needed for successful enrollment. Whether you are a new provider or managing a credentialing department, this guide will help you navigate the process with clarity, efficiency, and confidence.

Key Credentialing Components

Taxonomy Codes: Taxonomy codes are standardized codes used to classify healthcare providers and specialties based on the services they offer. These codes provide a systematic way to categorize healthcare professionals and ensure that they are appropriately credentialed for their specific roles. Each provider is assigned a taxonomy code that accurately reflects their area of expertise and practice.

National Provider Identifier (NPI): The National Provider Identifier (NPI) is a unique identification number assigned to healthcare providers in the United States. It serves as a standard identifier for healthcare transactions and is used by various entities, including health plans, providers, and patients. Obtaining an NPI is a fundamental requirement for credentialing healthcare providers and is necessary for billing, claims processing, and other administrative functions.

Council for Affordable Quality Healthcare (CAQH): The Council for Affordable Quality Healthcare (CAQH) is a nonprofit organization that streamlines the healthcare credentialing process through its Universal Provider Data Source (UPD) platform. Healthcare providers enroll in CAQH and submit their credentialing information, including licensure, education, and professional history. Health plans and credentialing organizations can access this information electronically, reducing administrative burdens and expediting the credentialing process.

Attestations: Attestations are statements or certifications provided by healthcare providers confirming their compliance with specific standards or requirements. These attestations may relate to professional qualifications, licensure, training, or adherence to ethical standards and regulations. Attestations play a crucial role in credentialing processes, as they demonstrate a provider's commitment to upholding quality and safety standards in healthcare delivery.

Importance of Credentialing Requirements

Credentialing requirements are essential for the following reasons:

Patient Safety: Credentialing ensures that healthcare providers meet minimum standards of competency and qualifications, thereby safeguarding patient safety and well-being. By verifying provider credentials, healthcare organizations mitigate risks associated with incompetent or unqualified practitioners.

Regulatory Compliance: Compliance with credentialing requirements is essential for healthcare organizations to meet regulatory standards and accreditation requirements. Failure to credential providers adequately can result in legal and financial consequences, including fines, litigation, and loss of accreditation.

Quality Assurance: Credentialing promotes quality assurance by ensuring that healthcare providers possess the necessary skills, training, and experience to deliver high-quality care. By maintaining rigorous credentialing standards, healthcare organizations uphold their commitment to excellence in patient care.

Insurance Reimbursement: Credentialing requirements, such as obtaining an NPI and enrolling in CAQH, are often prerequisites for insurance reimbursement. Healthcare providers must meet these requirements to participate in insurance networks and receive timely reimbursement for services rendered.

The Necessary Steps for Physicians and Staff to Become Credentialed with Insurance Companies

Credentialing with insurance companies is vital for physicians and healthcare staff seeking to provide medical services and receive reimbursement from insurance plans. Certification ensures that healthcare providers meet the insurer's requirements, including qualifications, licenses, and quality standards. This comprehensive guide outlines the necessary steps for physicians and staff to complete the credentialing process with insurance companies.

Companies: The Credentialing Process—Step-by-Step

The credentialing process can be visualized in the following flowchart:

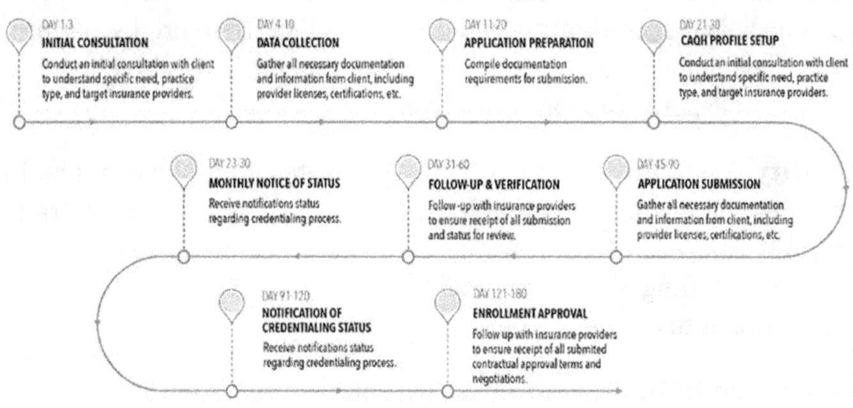

"Figure 4.1: Credentialing Process Overview"

Steps for Credentialing with Insurance Companies

Credentialing with insurance companies allows physicians and healthcare staff to provide services and receive reimbursement. Below is an overview of the process:

1. **Research and Select Insurance Plans:** The first step is to research the various insurance plans where the practice operates. Physicians and staff should assess the plans' network requirements, patient demographics, and reimbursement rates. Selecting

insurance plans that align with the practice's specialties and patient population is crucial for successful credentialing.

2. **Gather Required Documentation:** Insurance companies typically require specific documentation to evaluate a provider's qualifications. Common documents include:

    - Medical licenses and certifications
    - DEA registration (if applicable)
    - Malpractice insurance coverage
    - Board certifications (if relevant)
    - Education and training certificates
    - Work history and references
    - Curriculum vitae (CV) or résumé

3. **Complete Application Forms:** Each insurance plan has its own application forms for credentialing. Physicians and staff should carefully complete all required sections and provide accurate, up-to-date information. Consistency with the information supplied in the application and accompanying documentation must be ensured.

4. **Verify Credentialing Requirements:** Physicians and staff should verify the specific credentialing requirements of each insurance company. Some plans may have additional requirements, such as completing certain training programs or meeting specific patient volume criteria.

5. **Submit the Credentialing Application:** Upon completing the application and any supporting documentation, physicians and staff should submit them to insurance companies. The submission

can be made electronically through the insurer's credentialing portal or by mail, depending on the insurer's preference.

6. **Follow Up on Application Status:** Following up with the insurance companies is crucial to verify receipt of the application and learn the status of the credentialing procedure. This ensures the application is processed and helps identify missing or incomplete information.

7. **Respond to Requests for Additional Information:** Insurance companies may request additional information or clarification during the credentialing process. Physicians and staff should promptly respond to these requests and provide the necessary documents to avoid delays in the credentialing timeline.

8. **Enrollment Process:** Once the credentialing process is complete, physicians and staff must undergo the provider enrollment process with each insurance company. This process includes signing contracts and agreements outlining the terms of participation in the network.

9. **Attend Orientation and Training (if required):** Some insurance companies may require physicians and staff to attend orientation or training sessions to familiarize themselves with the plan's policies, billing procedures, and quality standards. Participation in such sessions is essential to ensure compliance with the insurer's guidelines.

10. **Update Credentialing Information Regularly:** Credentialing is not a one-time process. Physicians and staff must keep their credentialing information up to date by promptly notifying insurance companies of any changes in their practice, qualifications, or contact details.

11. **Monitor Contract Renewal Dates:** Insurance plan contracts have expiration dates. Physicians and staff should monitor these

dates and initiate the credentialing process well in advance to avoid disruptions in network participation.

12. **Be Patient and Persistent:** The credentialing process can be time-consuming, with varying processing times among insurance companies. Physicians and staff should remain patient and persistent throughout the process and be prepared to follow up with insurers as needed.
13. **Seek Professional Assistance:** Credentialing can be complex and time-consuming, especially for large healthcare practices or organizations. In such cases, seeking professional assistance from credentialing consultants can streamline the process and ensure compliance with all requirements.

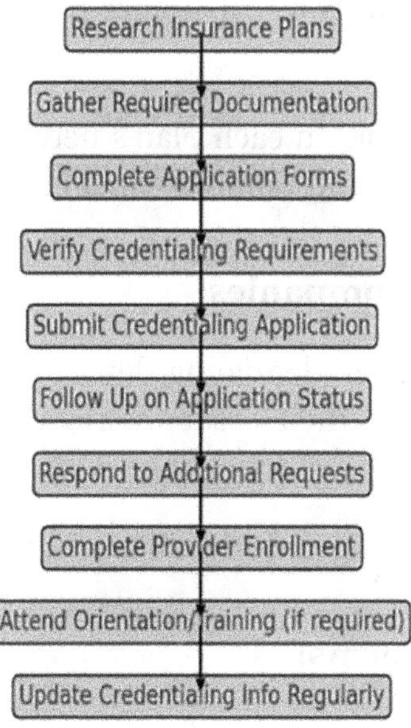

Figure 4.2: Credentialing Process Flowchart Overview

Checklist of Required Documents for Credentialing and Deadlines for Credentialing Submission

Credentialing with insurance companies involves thoroughly evaluating healthcare providers' qualifications and adherence to quality standards. To ensure a seamless and efficient credentialing process, physicians and healthcare staff must compile the necessary documents and meet specific deadlines for submission.

This comprehensive checklist outlines the required documents and associated deadlines for successful credentialing with insurance companies.

Credentialing Checklist

Research Insurance Plans:

□ Research and identify the insurance plans in which you wish to participate.

□ Gather information on each plan's network requirements, patient demographics, and reimbursement rates.

Contact Insurance Companies:

□ Reach out to the credentialing department of each insurance company to request their credentialing application and guidelines.

□ Inquire about any specific deadlines for submission.

Obtain Necessary Forms:

□ Obtain the credentialing application and required forms from each insurance company.

Personal Information:

□ Full legal name, contact information, and Social Security number.

□ Medical license number and expiration date.

□ National Provider Identifier (NPI) number.

□ Drug Enforcement Administration (DEA) registration (if applicable).

□ Malpractice insurance coverage details.

Education and Training Documents

□ Copies of medical school diploma and transcripts.

□ Board certifications and recertifications (if applicable).

□ Completed residency and fellowship certificates (if applicable).

□ Continuing Medical Education (CME) certificates.

Work History and References

□ Comprehensive work history, including previous employment, positions held, and dates of service.

□ Professional references, such as supervisors and colleagues.

Curriculum Vitae (CV) or Résumé

□ Prepare an updated CV or résumé outlining your educational background, professional experience, and relevant certifications.

State Licensing

□ Copies of current medical licenses for each state in which you practice.

Liability Insurance Certificate

□ Proof of malpractice insurance coverage with appropriate limits and expiration date.

Clinical Privileges and Hospital Affiliations

□ Documentation of clinical privileges granted by hospitals or healthcare facilities.

□ Affiliation letters from hospitals where you have staff privileges.

DEA Registration (if applicable)

□ Copy of DEA registration certificate for physicians prescribing controlled substances.

Provider Enrollment Application (CMS-855)

□ Complete and submit the CMS-855 application to the Centers for Medicare and Medicaid Services for Medicare participation.

Professional Liability Claims History

□ Complete and submit any required professional liability claims history forms.

Business Information (Group Practices)

□ Business name, tax identification number (TIN), and NPI for group practices.

Malpractice Claims History

□ Provide information on any past malpractice claims or lawsuits.

Peer References and Recommendations

□ Obtain letters of recommendation from colleagues and peers supporting your qualifications and clinical competence.

Certificate of Insurance (COI)

□ Provide proof of liability coverage in the form of a certificate of insurance.

Background Check Consent Form

□ Complete and sign a background check consent form allowing the insurance company to perform a background screening.

Signed Attestations

□ Sign and submit any required attestations regarding compliance with the insurance plan's policies and procedures.

Credentialing Application Fee

□ Submit the required credentialing application fee, if applicable.

Submission and Follow-Up Deadlines Checklist

Application Submission

□ Check the application submission deadline specified by each insurance company.

□ Be mindful of time frames. Late submissions may delay credentialing.

Follow-Up and Confirmation

□ Follow up with each insurance company to confirm receipt of your application and supporting documents.

□ Inquire about the expected processing time for your application.

Reverification and Recredentialing Deadlines

□ Track the deadlines for reverification and recredentialing, as these vary among insurance companies.

Contract Expiration

□ Note the contract expiration date with each insurance plan.

□ Initiate the credentialing renewal process well in advance to avoid disruptions.

Ongoing Updates

□ Maintain accurate records and promptly update your credentialing information to ensure continued compliance.

Benefits of Being Credentialed

Access to Insurance Networks: One of the primary benefits of being credentialed with insurance companies is gaining access to their provider networks. Being in-network allows healthcare providers to reach a broader patient base and attract new patients whose services are covered by their plans. In-network providers often enjoy a competitive advantage over out-of-network providers when it comes to patient referrals and visibility.

Increased Patient Trust: Credentialing gives patients assurance that the healthcare provider meets established standards of competency, education, and licensure. Patients are more likely to trust credentialed providers, which increases patient satisfaction and confidence in the care received.

Prompt and Timely Reimbursement: Credentialed providers experience faster and more consistent reimbursement from insurance companies. Credentialing ensures that billing and claims processes are streamlined, reducing payment delays and improving cash flow.

Compliance with Regulatory and Accreditation Standards: Being credentialed often requires adherence to specific regulatory and accreditation standards. Meeting these requirements reflects a provider's commitment to delivering quality care and complying with industry best practices.

Enhanced Professional Reputation: Credentialing adds to a provider's professional credibility and reputation within the healthcare community. It reflects a dedication to high standards and continued professional growth.

Collaborative Opportunities: Credentialing opens doors for collaboration with other healthcare professionals and organizations. Providers in the same network often refer patients to each other, supporting coordinated care.

Increased Revenue Potential: Credentialed providers can serve a larger patient base, which typically leads to increased patient volume and revenue growth for the practice.

Professional Development and Learning Opportunities: Many credentialing programs include continuing education requirements, encouraging healthcare providers to stay up to date on medical advancements and best practices that benefit both the provider and the patient.

Potential Pitfalls of Non-Compliance

Limited Patient Access: Non-compliant providers may be excluded from insurance networks, resulting in fewer referrals and reduced visibility. Patients often choose providers based on network participation, making compliance critical to access.

Delayed or Denied Payments: Providers who fail to meet credentialing requirements may experience delayed or denied claims. This can create financial strain and administrative challenges for the practice.

Loss of Competitive Advantage: Uncredentialed providers may be overlooked by patients and referring providers who prefer in-network or verified practitioners.

Legal and Regulatory Consequences: Failure to comply with credentialing requirements can lead to fines, loss of licensure, or legal action. Regulatory bodies hold practices accountable for credentialing compliance.

Negative Impact on Professional Reputation: Non-compliance can damage a provider's credibility and raise concerns about their commitment to industry standards and patient care quality.

Reduced Revenue Potential: A reduced patient base due to lack of network inclusion directly impacts income, limiting opportunities for growth and financial sustainability.

Limited Collaborative Opportunities: Providers outside of payer networks may be excluded from referral systems, partnerships, and shared care initiatives.

Stagnation of Professional Growth: Without meeting credentialing requirements, providers may miss out on opportunities for continuing education and professional advancement.

Frequently Asked Questions (FAQs)

Q: What is your educational background in credentialing?

A: Credentialing professionals often have education ranging from a high school diploma or credentialing certification (e.g., AAPC, NCQA, NAMSS CPCS) to a Master of Business Administration (MBA) or a doctorate in healthcare. Most clients seek credentialing partners with five or more years of experience.

Q: Are you familiar with payers in other states?

A: Yes. Credentialing providers typically submit applications to multiple state plans and understand the differences in payer requirements across regions.

Q: How long does the credentialing process take?

A: On average, 30 to 90 days, depending on the insurer and application complexity.

Steps include:

- Reviewing application materials for accuracy and completeness
- Verifying credentials and background
- Credentialing committee review
- Final approval and effective date confirmation

Q: What documents are required upfront?

A: TIN, NPI, taxonomy, education and licensure records, certifications, CV/résumé, background check authorization, and CAQH login credentials.

Q: What challenges do you typically see in businesses like mine?

A: Common issues include incomplete applications, missing documents, outdated CAQH profiles, or delays in provider follow-up. Accuracy and organization are key.

Q: How often will you work on my account and applications?

A: Credentialing support is typically ongoing, with weekly or monthly activity until paneling is complete.

Q: Will I need to re-credential?

A: Yes.

- Every 3 years for most commercial health plans
- Every 5 years for Medicare and Medicaid

Q: Do I need to be contracted for each payer or can I stay out-of-network?

A: You must be credentialed and contracted to be considered in-network. Out-of-network reimbursement depends on the patient's plan and may leave the patient with a higher financial burden.

Q: Does credentialing guarantee reimbursement?

A: No. Payment depends on eligibility, billing accuracy, coding compliance, and timely submission. Credentialing is only one part of the process.

Q: Why should I get credentialed?

A: It increases visibility, expands your patient base, enhances reputation, and supports long-term financial sustainability.

Q: Can I just work with a biller instead of getting credentialed?

A: No. Billing companies handle claims, but credentialing creates the legal relationship with payers that allows reimbursement. Providers must be enrolled to receive payment.

Q: How much will each payer reimburse me?

A: Reimbursement varies by payer and contract. Credentialing does not guarantee specific payment amounts.

Q: Do I need an NPI before credentialing?

A: Yes. An active NPI is required for enrollment and claims submission.

Q: Can an outdated CAQH profile delay approval?

A: Absolutely. Payers rely on your CAQH profile for real-time data. Keep it updated at all times.

Q: I'm leaving a group practice—does my credentialing transfer?

A: No. Credentialing is tied to the group and must be restarted when forming a new practice or going solo.

Chapter Reflection and Implementation Notes

What New Insights Did I Gain?

(Use this space to reflect on key takeaways from this chapter.)

How Can I Apply These Principles in My Practice?

(Note actionable steps or ideas inspired by this chapter.)

Additional Notes

(Use the lines below for any further notes, ideas, or observations.)

CHAPTER 5
REVIEWING EOBs (EXPLANATION OF BENEFITS)

Understanding Your Healthcare Coverage and Costs

Explanations of Benefits (EOBs) are essential documents that provide detailed information about the healthcare services a patient has received and the associated costs. Insurance companies send EOBs to policyholders and healthcare providers to explain how claims were processed, what services were covered, and what portion of the cost is the patient's responsibility.

Reviewing EOBs is a crucial part of understanding healthcare coverage, identifying billing errors, and managing costs effectively. This chapter explains the key components of EOBs and provides tips on how to review and interpret them accurately.

Why Reviewing EOBs Is Important

Understanding Healthcare Costs: EOBs break down the costs of healthcare services, including the amount billed by the provider, the insurance company's approved amount, any deductibles or co-payments, and the patient's financial responsibility. Patients must review their EOBs to understand their obligations and make informed choices about their healthcare expenditures.

Identifying Billing Errors: EOBs allow providers to verify the accuracy of the billed services and the amounts charged. Reviewing EOBs helps identify errors such as duplicate charges or services not covered by the plan. Detecting and resolving errors promptly can prevent unnecessary costs and potential disputes with healthcare providers.

Monitoring Insurance Coverage: Regularly reviewing EOBs helps ensure that claims are processed correctly and that insurance obligations are being met. Any denials or discrepancies can be addressed promptly to avoid unexpected out-of-pocket expenses.

Managing Healthcare Expenses: By understanding their EOBs, healthcare practices can better manage expenses and budget for future treatments. EOBs provide insight into the cost of services, which can inform planning and decision-making.

Enhancing Healthcare Literacy: Reviewing EOBs offers an opportunity to improve healthcare literacy. Understanding the terminology and codes used in EOBs empowers providers and patients to engage in meaningful conversations with insurers and providers.

Key Components of an EOB

- **Patient Information:** Includes the patient's name, policy number, and relationship to the policyholder (e.g., spouse, dependent).
- **Service Details:** Describes the healthcare services rendered, including the date of service, provider or facility name, and service type.
- **Provider Charges:** Outlines the total amount billed by the provider for the services rendered.

- **Allowed Amount:** Indicates the maximum amount the insurance will pay for a covered service, usually based on the contracted rate.
- **Deductible:** The portion the patient must pay out of pocket before the insurer begins covering expenses. The EOB shows the amount applied to the deductible and the remaining balance.
- **Co-payment and Coinsurance:** Specifies the patient's share, either as a fixed co-payment or a percentage (coinsurance) of the allowed amount.
- **Insurance Payment:** Shows how much the insurance company paid toward the service.
- **Patient Responsibility:** Details what the patient owes, including co-payments, coinsurance, deductibles, and any non-covered services.
- **Claim Status:** Indicates whether the claim was paid, denied, or is pending. If denied, the EOB will often explain why and outline appeal procedures.
- **Summary of Benefits:** Some EOBs include a summary of the patient's plan benefits, deductible progress, out-of-pocket maximums, and services covered.

Tips for Reviewing EOBs

- **Review Promptly:** Examine EOBs as soon as they arrive to address any issues or discrepancies immediately.

- **Compare with Medical Bills:** Cross-check EOBs against the provider's bills to ensure consistency in billed services and insurance payments.
- **Understand Insurance Terminology:** Learn common insurance terms and codes to better interpret EOB details and patient obligations.
- **Keep EOBs Organized:** Maintain a record of all EOBs for reference, especially in case of audits, tax deductions, or disputes.
- **Contact the Insurance Company for Clarification:** If anything is unclear, reach out to the insurer's customer service for a detailed explanation.
- **Appeal Denials if Necessary:** If a claim is denied, follow the appeal steps outlined in the EOB and submit any required documentation.
- **Seek Professional Assistance:** For complex issues, billing discrepancies, or unclear terminology, consult with an insurance expert or healthcare billing professional.

The Importance of Reviewing EOBs for Accuracy and Understanding

The Explanation of Benefits (EOB) is a critical document in healthcare billing, outlining the services provided, the amount billed, and the portion covered by insurance. While patients often receive and review their EOBs, it is equally essential for providers and office staff to understand and accurately review these documents. This practice ensures correct billing, maximizes reimbursement, and maintains transparent communication with patients.

Ensuring Billing Accuracy

Prevent Billing Errors

Reviewing EOBs helps identify and correct billing errors. Providers and office staff should compare EOB details with medical records and service invoices. Discrepancies may result from coding errors, incorrect service dates, or miscommunication with insurance companies. Catching these errors early prevents revenue loss and supports the integrity of billing practices.

Verify Services Rendered

Office staff should confirm that the services listed on the EOB were indeed rendered. This step ensures the billing reflects actual care provided and aids in detecting fraudulent claims. Accurate verification also supports proper documentation, which is crucial for audits and regulatory compliance.

Maximizing Reimbursement

Understand Insurance Coverage

Providers and office staff must understand the nuances of different insurance plans and what they cover. Reviewing EOBs keeps staff informed about coverage limits, co-pays, deductibles, and denied services. This knowledge allows staff to optimize billing practices, ensuring all billable services are claimed and potential denials are addressed proactively.

Appeal Denied Claims

Denied claims are a common challenge in healthcare billing. By thoroughly reviewing EOBs, staff can determine the reason for denials, such as coding errors or insufficient medical necessity documentation. Understanding these reasons allows staff to file timely and effective appeals, which can recover significant revenue.

Enhancing Patient Communication

Transparent Communication

Educated and informed staff are better equipped to explain EOB details to patients, improving transparency and trust. Patients often have questions about what services were covered, their financial responsibility, and any discrepancies they observe. Well-informed staff can provide clear, accurate explanations, enhancing overall patient satisfaction.

Proactive Issue Resolution

By regularly reviewing EOBs, staff can identify and address potential issues before they escalate. For instance, if a patient is likely to receive a large bill due to insurance denial, staff can inform the patient in advance and explore solutions such as payment plans or resubmission with additional documentation.

Maintaining Compliance and Avoiding Legal Issues

Regulatory Compliance

Accurate EOB review ensures compliance with healthcare regulations and payer policies. Noncompliance can lead to penalties, audits, or legal action. Office staff must be well-versed in the relevant regulations to uphold adherence and mitigate risks.

Documentation and Record-Keeping

Proper review and understanding of EOBs contribute to meticulous record-keeping. This is crucial during audits and for legal compliance. Maintaining detailed records of services rendered, billing history, and communications with insurance companies provides a strong defense against potential disputes.

Sample EOB Walkthrough: Explanation of Key Sections and Terminology

To better understand the structure and terminology of an Explanation of Benefits (EOB), let's review a sample EOB for a fictional patient, John Smith. John recently visited a healthcare provider for a routine medical check-up. The EOB provided by his insurance company summarizes how the claim was processed:

Section	Details
Patient Information	**Name:** John Smith, **Patient ID:** 123456789, **Policy Number:** XYZ-12345
Service Details	**Service Date:** 2023-06-15, **Service:** Routine Check-up, **Provider:** ABC Medical Clinic
Provider Charges	**Total Billed:** $250.00, **Allowed Amount:** $180.00, **Discount:** $70.00

Section	Details
Deductible & Co-pay	**Deductible:** $100.00, **Co-payment:** $20.00
Insurance Payment	**Amount Paid by Insurance:** $160.00
Patient Responsibility	**Amount Due:** $40.00 (includes co-pay and remaining deductible)
Claim Status	**Status:** Paid
Summary of Benefits	**Deductible Remaining:** $60.00, **Out-of-Pocket Max:** $40.00

Key Components of EOBs

Understanding each section of the Explanation of Benefits (EOB) helps providers and staff interpret billing outcomes and improve communication with patients. Below is a detailed breakdown of the components using a sample EOB for a fictional patient, John Smith.

Section 1: Patient Information

This section lists John's personal and insurance details, including his name, patient ID (a unique identifier), policy number, and group number. These identifiers help insurance companies match the claim to the correct policyholder and ensure accurate processing.

Section 2: Service Details

This area specifies the date of the healthcare visit, June 15, 2023, the type of service rendered (routine medical check-up), and the provider's name (ABC Medical Clinic). It also includes the National Provider Identifier (NPI), a unique 10-digit number used to identify healthcare practitioners.

Section 3: Provider Charges

- Total Billed Charges: $250.00
- Allowed Amount: $180.00
- Discount Amount: $70.00

This section details the original amount billed by the provider, the insurance company's allowable charge, and the discount (difference between the two). In this case, John's provider billed $250.00, but the insurance allowed $180.00, applying a $70.00 discount.

Section 4: Deductible and Co-payment

- Deductible: $100.00
- Co-payment: $20.00

John's deductible is the out-of-pocket amount he must pay before insurance coverage applies. His co-payment is a fixed fee owed at the time of service.

Section 5: Insurance Payment

- Amount Paid by Insurance: $160.00

This reflects the payment made by the insurance provider toward John's routine medical check-up.

Section 6: Patient Responsibility

- Amount Due: $40.00

This section combines the co-payment and any remaining deductible. John owes $40.00, based on his insurance coverage and the allowed charge.

Section 7: Claim Status

- Status: Paid

This indicates the outcome of the claim. "Paid" means the insurance company processed the claim and remitted payment accordingly.

Section 8: Summary of Benefits

- Deductible Remaining: $60.00 (of $100.00)
- Out-of-Pocket Maximum Remaining: $40.00 (of $1,000.00)

This summary helps patients understand how much of their deductible and out-of-pocket maximum has been met.

Section 9: Contact Information

- Customer Service: 1-800-555-1234
- Website: www.insuranceco.com

Contact information is provided in case patients need assistance or clarification regarding their EOB or policy.

Guidance on Addressing Discrepancies or Denials

Addressing discrepancies or denials in healthcare claims is critical for maintaining accuracy, maximizing reimbursement, and ensuring a smooth revenue cycle. The steps below guide office staff through systematic resolution.

Understanding Discrepancies and Denials

- *Discrepancies* occur when information on the EOB does not align with medical records or the services provided. These may include incorrect codes, mismatched dates, or patient identification errors.
- *Denials* result when an insurance company refuses to pay a claim. Common reasons include missing preauthorization, coding issues, insufficient documentation, or lack of medical necessity.

Steps to Address Discrepancies

1. **Identify and Categorize Discrepancies**
    - *Regular Audits:* Routinely compare EOBs to patient records and billing statements.
    - *Categorization:* Group discrepancies by type (e.g., coding error, data mismatch) to streamline resolution.
2. **Correcting Errors**
    - *Data Verification:* Confirm accuracy of billing system entries. Check the patient data, service codes, and dates.

- *Code Correction:* Update inaccurate codes using the latest CPT/ICD guidelines. Ensure staff are trained on current coding standards.

3. **Communication and Documentation**
   - *Internal Communication:* Coordinate with billing and clinical staff to clarify services rendered.
   - *Documentation:* Log all corrections and actions taken for audit and compliance purposes.

Steps to Address Denials

1. **Denial Analysis**
   - *Reason Identification:* Examine denial notices to determine cause, whether coding, documentation, or policy related.
   - *Trend Analysis:* Track recurring denials to detect systemic issues in billing or documentation.
2. **Appeal Preparation**
   - *Gather Documentation:* Collect supporting documents such as medical records, treatment plans, and provider notes.
   - *Detailed Appeal Letter:* Draft a customized letter that addresses the specific denial reason, includes documentation, and references payer policies or medical necessity.

3. **Timely Submission**

    - *Adhere to Timelines:* Submit appeals within the required time frame. Late appeals are often automatically rejected.

    - *Follow-Up:* Track appeal status and document all correspondence for accountability.

Preventive Measures

Preauthorization and Verification

- *Preauthorization:* Create a checklist for procedures requiring prior approval. Confirm all authorizations before appointments.

- *Insurance Verification:* Always confirm a patient's insurance eligibility, co-pays, and coverage details before delivering services.

Training and Education

- *Staff Training:* Offer ongoing education on billing protocols, coding updates, and payer policy changes.

- *Coding Accuracy:* Employ certified coders or provide certification opportunities to improve billing accuracy.

Effective Communication

- *Patient Communication:* Clearly explain costs, coverage limits, and patient responsibility to reduce confusion and disputes.

- *Provider Communication:* Ensure accurate documentation by providers to support claim submissions and appeals.

Utilize Technology

- *Electronic Health Records (EHR):* Use EHR systems to streamline documentation and reduce entry errors.
- *Billing Software:* Invest in tools that detect errors and potential denials before claim submission. Automation reduces the risk of manual mistakes.

Chapter Reflection and Implementation Notes

What New Insights Did I Gain?

(Use this space to reflect on key takeaways from this chapter.)

How Can I Apply These Principles in My Practice?

(Note actionable steps or ideas inspired by this chapter.)

Additional Notes

(Use the lines below for any further notes, ideas, or observations.)

CHAPTER 6
VERIFYING CLAIM DENIALS

Verifying Claim Denials: Understanding Reasons, Appealing, and Resolving Disputes

Claim denials can be frustrating for both patients and healthcare providers. It is important to note that insurance companies may decline coverage for specific healthcare services or procedures. This can result in a claim denial, leaving the patient responsible for the expenses. These denials can occur for various reasons, including coding errors, lack of preauthorization, out-of-network services, and policy limitations. Verifying claim denials is a critical step in healthcare billing to ensure accurate reimbursement and fair patient coverage.

Importance of Verifying Claim Denials

Verification of claim denials is an absolute necessity for both patients and healthcare providers for several reasons:

Accuracy of Billing: Verifying denials ensures that claims are processed and paid correctly. Identifying and correcting errors early prevents inaccuracies and potential financial disputes.

Fair Coverage: Patients are entitled to receive coverage for services included in their insurance plan. Verifying denials ensures they receive the benefits they are due and helps avoid unnecessary out-of-pocket expenses.

Optimal Reimbursement: Healthcare providers rely on accurate claim processing for proper reimbursement. Verifying denials allows providers to address billing issues promptly and receive fair compensation.

Patient Satisfaction: Promptly addressing claim denials enhances patient satisfaction. Providers should advocate for their patients' interests to resolve billing disputes and maintain trust.

The Appeal Process

Patients and healthcare providers can appeal the decision when a claim is denied. The appeal process allows them to contest the denial and provide additional information to support the claim. The following steps are usually involved in the appeals process:

1. **Review the Denial Explanation:** The Explanation of Benefits (EOB) or denial letter from the insurance company will provide information about the reason for the denial. Review this explanation carefully to understand the basis of the denial.

2. **Gather Relevant Documentation:** To support the appeal, gather all relevant documentation, including medical records, test results, preauthorization documentation, and any other evidence that validates the necessity of the service.

3. **Complete the Appeal Form:** The insurance company may provide an appeal form or specific instructions for submitting an appeal. Follow the instructions carefully and provide all required information accurately.

4. **Submit the Appeal:** Send the completed appeal form and supporting documentation to the designated address or department specified by the insurance company. Ensure the appeal is submitted within the required timeframe to be considered valid.

5. **Follow Up:** After submitting the appeal, follow up with the insurance company to confirm receipt and inquire about the status of the appeal. Be prepared to provide any additional information or documentation the insurer may request.

6. **Escalate if Necessary:** If the appeal is denied at the initial level, inquire about additional levels of appeal. Some insurance companies have multiple levels of review, and the process may involve escalating the request to a higher authority.

Resolving Disputes Effectively

Resolving claim denials efficiently requires clear communication and persistence. Here are some tips for resolving disputes effectively:

- **Be Proactive:** Address denials as soon as possible to avoid delays in reimbursement and potential disputes.
- **Keep Records:** Maintain detailed records of all communications, including dates, representative names, and summaries of conversations with the insurance company.
- **Understand the Insurance Policy:** Familiarize yourself with the terms and conditions of the insurance policy to ensure that services are covered and preauthorization requirements are met.
- **Seek Assistance if Needed:** If the appeal process becomes complex or overwhelming, consider seeking assistance from a revenue cycle consultant or legal professional.
- **Communicate Clearly:** When contacting the insurance company, provide all relevant information clearly and concisely.

- **Be Persistent:** Follow up regularly on the appeal status and stay persistent until the issue is resolved.
- **Be Patient:** Resolving claim denials can take time. Remain patient throughout the process.

Guide for Physicians and Staff on Identifying Claim Denials

Identifying claim denials and understanding the reasons for rejection are crucial tasks for physicians and staff involved in the healthcare billing process. Claim denials can lead to delays in reimbursement, increased administrative burden, and dissatisfied patients. By proactively identifying discrepancies and addressing their underlying causes, healthcare providers can streamline their revenue cycle, improve billing accuracy, and enhance patient satisfaction.

This guide offers physicians and staff practical steps to identify claim denials, recognize common reasons for rejection, and implement strategies to prevent and resolve these issues efficiently.

Steps to Manage Claim Denials

1. **Establish Effective Claim Tracking Systems:** The first step in identifying claim denials is implementing an effective claim-tracking system. Utilize electronic health records (EHR) or practice management software that enables staff to monitor claims from submission through reimbursement. A centralized system helps track claims in real time and quickly identifies denials.
2. **Regularly Monitor Claims:** Consistent monitoring of submitted claims is essential. Assign staff members to monitor claims daily or weekly, depending on claim volume. This ensures denials

are identified promptly, preventing unnecessary delays in reimbursement.

3. **Familiarize with Common Denial Codes:** Healthcare providers and billing staff should be well-versed in the standard denial codes used by insurance companies. These codes provide insight into the specific reason for the denial, such as coding errors, lack of preauthorization, or policy limitations. Understanding these codes facilitates faster resolution.

4. **Analyze Denial Patterns:** Track and review denial patterns to identify recurring issues. Look for trends in services or procedures frequently denied, or specific payers that issue denials consistently. Recognizing these patterns allows providers to focus corrective efforts and reduce future denials.

5. **Collaborate with Billing Teams:** Effective communication between providers and billing teams is essential. Physicians should inform billing staff of any services requiring preauthorization or unique billing requirements. This collaborative approach reduces denials caused by missing information or procedural missteps.

6. **Ensure Accurate Coding:** Accurate coding is critical in preventing denials. Train staff on current coding standards and guidelines. Conduct regular pre-submission claim reviews to verify codes and confirm that supporting documentation is complete and compliant.

7. **Verify Eligibility and Coverage:** Before providing services, verify patient eligibility and insurance benefits. Ensure the services being rendered are covered by the patient's plan. This step helps avoid denials due to non-covered services or policy exclusions.

8. **Prioritize Preauthorization:** For services requiring prior approval, make preauthorization a top priority. Missed or delayed preauthorization is a common reason for claim denials. Develop a

streamlined process to request and confirm authorizations before service delivery.

9. **Address Timely Filing Limits:** Insurance companies enforce strict deadlines for claim submissions. Ensure that all claims are filed within the allowable timeframe to avoid automatic denials for late filing.

10. **Implement Quality Assurance Measures:** Establish quality checks to review claims before submission. Use a checklist to verify all required information is included and properly documented. This minimizes avoidable errors and reduces the likelihood of denial.

11. **Track Denied Claims:** Maintain a log or spreadsheet tracking denied claims, including the reason for denial. Monitoring this information helps identify systemic problems and focus resolution efforts where they're most needed.

12. **Communicate with Insurance Companies:** Maintain open and consistent communication with insurance representatives. Timely dialogue helps clarify claim issues and accelerates resolution, minimizing reimbursement delays.

13. **Follow Up on Appeals:** If a claim is denied and an appeal is submitted, follow up regularly to monitor its status. Stay informed about the process and provide additional information as requested by the insurer.

14. **Educate Staff on Denial Prevention:** Conduct ongoing training for staff on topics such as billing practices, insurance policy updates, and coding changes. Regular education strengthens your team's ability to submit clean claims and prevent denials.

15. **Seek Expert Assistance if Needed:** In complex or persistent denial situations, consider enlisting revenue cycle management

consultants or billing specialists. These experts offer insights and tools to resolve ongoing issues and improve future claim success.

The Process of Appealing Denied Claims

Appealing denied claims involves challenging an insurance company's decision to deny reimbursement for specific healthcare services or procedures. Submitting an appeal is a necessary step to contest a denial, and it must be accompanied by substantial evidence or documentation that strengthens the claim. The appeal process gives healthcare providers and patients the opportunity to correct errors, submit missing documentation, or clarify misunderstandings that contributed to the denial.

Below is a step-by-step guide on how to appeal denied claims:

Step 1: Review the Denial Explanation

When a claim is denied, begin by carefully reviewing the Explanation of Benefits (EOB) or the denial letter provided by the insurance company. These documents include the reason for denial, such as coding errors, lack of preauthorization, or policy limitations. Understanding the specific reason for the rejection is essential for preparing an effective appeal.

Step 2: Gather Supporting Documentation

Collect all necessary records and documentation to support your appeal. This may include medical records, test results, preauthorization documentation, and any other materials that demonstrate the medical necessity of the service provided. The goal is to present a thorough case showing that the denied claim meets the insurance company's coverage criteria.

Step 3: Complete the Appeal Form

Many insurance companies provide an appeal form specifically for this purpose. If an appeal form is not available, draft a formal appeal letter. Be sure to include the patient's full name, policy number, claim number, date of service, and a clear explanation of why the claim should be reconsidered. Attach all supporting documentation to the appeal letter or form.

Step 4: Submit the Appeal

Send the completed appeal form or letter, along with the necessary documentation, to the designated address or department listed by the insurance company. Be sure to submit the appeal within the insurer's required timeframe. Most insurance companies have strict deadlines, and appeals filed late are often denied automatically.

Step 5: Follow Up

After the appeal has been submitted, follow up with the insurance company to confirm that the appeal was received and to inquire about the review status. Keep a detailed record of all communication, including dates, times, names of representatives, and summaries of each discussion.

Step 6: Review the Appeal Response

Once the insurance company processes the appeal, it will issue a response. The appeal may be approved, resulting in reimbursement, or denied again. If the appeal is successful, the insurer will usually issue payment promptly and provide an updated EOB.

Further Steps

If the initial appeal is denied, check with the insurance company to determine whether additional levels of appeal are available. Some insurers allow multiple appeal levels, which may escalate the case to another department or involve an independent review panel.

Tips for a Successful Appeal

- **Be timely:** Submit the appeal within the required timeframe to prevent automatic denial due to late filing.
- **Be thorough:** Provide all relevant information and complete supporting documentation to strengthen your case.
- **Be clear:** Clearly state your reasons for the appeal and outline why you believe the claim should be approved.
- **Be persistent:** Continue to follow up on the status of your appeal and be ready to supply additional information if requested.
- **Seek assistance if needed:** If the appeal process becomes overwhelming or complex, consider consulting a revenue cycle management expert or billing consultant for guidance.

Step-by-Step Process for Preparing a Medical Claim Appeal

Preparing a medical claim appeal is a detailed and crucial process for healthcare providers and patients seeking to challenge a denied claim. An appeal provides an opportunity to request reconsideration of the denial by submitting additional information and evidence that support the claim's validity. A well-structured and thoroughly documented request can significantly increase the likelihood of a successful outcome.

This guide outlines a step-by-step process to effectively prepare a medical claim appeal:

Step 1: Review the Denial Explanation

Begin by carefully reviewing the Explanation of Benefits (EOB) or denial letter provided by the insurance company. Identify the specific reason for the denial, such as coding errors, lack of preauthorization, or policy limitations. A clear understanding of the basis for the denial forms the foundation of a compelling appeal.

Step 2: Gather Supporting Documentation

Collect all relevant documentation to strengthen your appeal. This may include medical records, test results, referral letters, preauthorization documentation, and any other evidence that supports the medical necessity of the services provided. Ensure that all documents are complete, well organized, and easy to reference.

Step 3: Identify the Appropriate Appeal Level

Determine the appropriate level of appeal based on the insurance company's established process. Insurers typically offer multiple levels of appeal, each with specific requirements and submission deadlines.

Identifying the correct level ensures compliance and helps streamline the appeal.

Step 4: Obtain the Appeal Form or Template

If the insurance company provides an appeal form or template, obtain it and fill it out accurately. If no form is available, draft a formal appeal letter that includes all necessary details such as the patient's full name, policy number, claim number, date of service, and the specific reason for the appeal.

Step 5: Craft the Appeal Letter

When drafting the appeal letter, be clear and concise in stating the appeal's basis. Directly address the denial's stated reason and provide an explanation of why the claim should be reconsidered. Support your points with relevant facts, references, and documentation.

Step 6: Use Appropriate Terminology and Codes

Incorporate proper medical terminology and standardized coding in the appeal letter. Demonstrating clinical accuracy and aligning your language with accepted coding systems can increase the appeal's credibility and improve its chances of being approved.

Step 7: Present a Strong Argument

Construct a well-reasoned argument explaining why the service was medically necessary, met the insurer's coverage criteria, and should not have been denied. Focus on factual, logical reasoning supported by documentation.

Step 8: Address Each Denial Reason

If multiple reasons were cited for the denial, address each one separately in the appeal letter. Clearly explain how each issue has been resolved or how the original submission met the insurer's criteria.

Step 9: Include Relevant Guidelines and Policies

Reference relevant insurance company policies, benefit guidelines, or criteria for medical necessity that support your appeal. Demonstrating that the claim falls within covered services as defined by the insurer reinforces your position.

Step 10: Attach Supporting Documentation

Attach all gathered documentation, such as medical records, test results, and preauthorization approvals. Clearly label each attachment and reference it in your letter to ensure it supports your claims logically and sequentially.

Step 11: Submit the Appeal

Send the completed appeal letter and all accompanying documentation to the address or department specified by the insurance company. Be sure to follow submission instructions precisely and verify that the appeal is submitted within the required timeframe.

Step 12: Keep a Record of the Appeal

Maintain a detailed record of the entire appeal process. Document the submission date, the name of the insurance contact person, and summaries of all communications. Retaining thorough records helps support future correspondence or additional appeal efforts.

Step 13: Follow Up on the Appeal

After submission, follow up with the insurance company to confirm receipt and check the status of the appeal. Be persistent and responsive to any requests for additional information or clarification.

Step 14: Review the Appeal Response

Once a decision has been made, review the insurance company's response carefully. If the appeal is successful and the denial is overturned, verify that the claim is being processed and that payment is issued according to the updated decision.

Step 15: Further Steps if Denied

If the appeal is denied at the initial level, inquire about the next available level of appeal. Many insurance companies allow for multiple rounds of review, including escalation to an independent or external review body.

Chapter Reflection and Implementation Notes

What New Insights Did I Gain?

(Use this space to reflect on key takeaways from this chapter.)

How Can I Apply These Principles in My Practice?

(Note actionable steps or ideas inspired by this chapter.)

Additional Notes

(Use the lines below for any further notes, ideas, or observations.)

CHAPTER 7
HOW TO APPEAL MEDICAL CLAIMS TEMPLATE

The process of appealing medical claims can be overwhelming and frustrating, but it is a necessary step to ensure you receive the rightful coverage for your medical expenses. Whether you are a patient or a healthcare provider, understanding how to appeal medical claims effectively is crucial in obtaining fair reimbursement.

Appeals are often triggered by claim denials due to billing errors, lack of preauthorization, insufficient documentation, or policy exclusions. Left unaddressed, these denials can result in significant financial burdens or lost revenue. However, with the right approach and tools, the appeals process becomes a manageable and strategic opportunity to correct discrepancies, clarify medical necessity, and advocate for coverage.

This chapter provides a clear, adaptable template for writing an effective medical claim appeal letter. The structure can be used across a variety of scenarios and payer requirements. Whether submitting to a private insurer, Medicare, or Medicaid, the principles of a strong appeal remain the same: be thorough, timely, professional, and persistent.

Use the following guidance and template to streamline your appeals and improve your chances of a successful outcome.

Sample Medical Claim Appeal Letter Template

Below is a template you can use when crafting your appeal letter. Be sure to customize the details to your specific case.

[Your Name]
[Your Address]
[City, State, ZIP]
[Your Phone Number]
[Your Email Address]
[Date]

[Insurance Company Name]
Claims Department
[Address]
[City, State, ZIP]

Subject: Appeal for Claim Denial [Claim Number/Reference]

Dear [Insurance Company Representative's Name],

I am writing to formally appeal the denial of the claim referenced above, submitted on [Date]. After reviewing the Explanation of Benefits (EOB) received on [Date], I believe the denial was issued in error, and I respectfully request a thorough reevaluation of my claim.

Patient Information:

Patient's Full Name: [Full Name]

Patient's Date of Birth: [Date of Birth]

Patient's Insurance ID: [Insurance ID]

Claim Number: [Claim Number]

Date of Service: [Date of Service]

Reason for Denial:

According to the EOB, the claim was denied for the following reason: [state the denial reason as listed in the EOB, e.g., "Lack of medical necessity," "Out-of-network service"].

Grounds for Appeal:

I believe that this denial is unjustified for the following reasons:

Medical Necessity:

The services provided were medically necessary for diagnosing and treating my condition. [Provide a brief explanation of the medical necessity, citing specific health concerns or symptoms.]

Insurance Policy Coverage:

After reviewing my insurance policy [policy number], I have confirmed that the services in question are covered under the terms of the policy. The denial does not align with the coverage provided in my plan. [Reference specific sections of your insurance policy.]

Supporting Documentation:

I have enclosed supporting documentation, including medical records, physician notes, test results, and itemized bills, which clearly demonstrate the medical necessity of the services rendered and their eligibility for coverage.

Coding Accuracy:

I believe the denial may have resulted from coding errors. Please review the coding to ensure that all services were appropriately billed.

Pre-Authorization:

Pre-authorization was obtained for the services rendered, as required by my insurance policy. A copy of the pre-authorization confirmation is enclosed for your reference.

Request for Reevaluation: Given the above information and the supporting documentation, I respectfully request that you reevaluate my claim and reverse the denial decision. I seek a fair and impartial reconsideration of the claim's merits.

Thank you for your attention to this matter. Please feel free to contact me at [Your Phone Number] or [Your Email Address] should you need any further information or clarification.

Sincerely,

[Your Name]
[Your Signature] (if mailing a physical copy)

Key Elements to Include in Your Appeal Letter

An effective appeal letter for a medical claim denial should be well-structured and include essential elements to present a persuasive case. Here are the key factors that must be included in the appeal letter:

Patient Information: Begin the letter by providing the patient's full name, Date of birth, insurance ID, claim number, and the Date of service for the denied claim. This information helps the insurance company identify the case and ensures the appeal is directed to the correct recipient.

Date of Denial and Claim Details: State the Date on which the claim was denied and include the relevant claim details, such as the type of service, CPT (Current Procedural Terminology) or procedure codes, and the billed amount. Mention the claim number referenced in the Explanation of Benefits (EOB).

Denial Reason: Explicitly mention the reason given by the insurance company for the claim denial. This information is usually found in the Explanation of Benefits (EOB) you received. Knowing the exact denial reason will help you address the specific issue in your appeal.

Grounds for Appeal: Explain why you believe the denial is unjustified. You should provide a well-reasoned argument, citing the relevant information that supports your case. The grounds for appeal can include factors such as medical necessity, coverage under the insurance policy, coding accuracy, pre-authorization, or other relevant information that may have been overlooked during the initial review.

Supporting Documentation: Include all relevant supporting documents that back up your appeal's claims. This may include medical records, physician notes, test results, itemized bills, pre-authorization confirmation, and other relevant documents. Ensure the documents are organized, legible, and referenced within the appeal letter.

Insurance Policy Coverage: Reference the specific section of your insurance policy that supports your claim for coverage. Explain how the services rendered align with the covered benefits and limitations outlined in the policy. This demonstrates that the requested services should be eligible for reimbursement.

Request for Reevaluation: Clearly state that you are appealing the denial and formally request a thorough reevaluation of your claim. Emphasize that you seek a fair and impartial reconsideration of the claim's merits.

Polite and Professional Tone: Maintaining a strictly professional and respectful tone in the letter is essential. Avoid emotional language or accusations. A courteous approach enhances the chances of a positive response from the insurance company and increases the credibility of your appeal.

Contact Information: Include your contact details (phone and email) to facilitate communication during the review process. The insurance company can easily reach you for additional information or clarification.

Signature: End the letter with your handwritten signature if sending a physical copy. For digital submissions, a typed signature will suffice.

Tips for Writing an Effective and Persuasive Appeal Letter

Here are some tips to help you craft a compelling appeal letter:

Be Prompt: Submit your appeal letter as soon as possible after receiving the denial. Many insurance companies have specific deadlines for filing appeals, so act promptly to make sure you get the window for request.

Address the Recipient Properly: Use the appropriate salutation and address the letter to the individual or department responsible for appeals. Find the name of the person in charge of requests to add a personal touch to the letter.

Keep It Concise and Focused: Be clear and concise in your arguments. Avoid unnecessary details and tangents that may detract from the main points. State the letter's purpose up front and stick to the relevant information supporting your case.

Provide Specific Details: Include details about the denied claim, such as the patient's information, claim number, Date of service, and the denial reason. Referencing these details makes your appeal more organized and understandable.

Clearly State the Grounds for Appeal: Explain why you believe the denial is unjustified. Use facts, evidence, and relevant references to support your case. Address the specific denial reason and provide counterarguments.

Reference Your Insurance Policy: If the denial is related to coverage, refer to the specific sections of your insurance policy that support your claim. Highlight the language that indicates the services that should be covered.

Attach Supporting Documents: Attach all relevant supporting documents, such as medical records, physician notes, test results, and itemized bills. These documents provide evidence to back up your appeal's claims.

Organize Information Effectively: Present your arguments in a logical and organized manner. Use headings or bullet points to make the letter easy to read and navigate.

Be Persuasive but Not Argumentative: While you should advocate for your rights, avoid sounding confrontational or argumentative. Focus on presenting a solid case supported by evidence and rationale.

Demonstrate Medical Necessity: If the denial is based on medical necessity, clearly explain why the services were necessary for your health and well-being. Provide medical evidence to support your claims.

Appeal to Fairness and Common Sense: If applicable, appeal to the insurance company's sense of fairness and logic. Explain why it is reasonable for them to cover the services in question.

Proofread: Ensure the letter is free of grammatical errors and typographical mistakes. A well-written letter shows attention to detail and professionalism.

Follow Any Specific Instructions: If the insurance company has provided guidelines for appeals, follow them meticulously. Adhering to their requirements demonstrates respect for their process.

Keep Copies: Make copies of your appeal letter and all supporting documents for your records. This ensures you have a complete description of your submission.

Be Persistent: If you have yet to receive a response within a reasonable period, contact the insurance provider to enquire about the status of your appeal. Be persistent in seeking updates.

Key Elements to Include in Your Appeal Letter

An effective appeal letter for a medical claim denial should be well-structured and include all essential elements to present a persuasive case. The following components should be included:

Patient Information: Begin by providing the patient's full name, date of birth, insurance ID number, claim number, and the date of service associated with the denied claim. This information allows the insurance company to locate the correct file and ensures the appeal is directed appropriately.

Date of Denial and Claim Details: Clearly state the date on which the claim was denied and include all relevant claim details. This should include the type of service rendered, associated CPT (Current Procedural Terminology) or procedure codes, and the total amount billed. Reference the claim number as it appears on the Explanation of Benefits (EOB).

Denial Reason: Explicitly state the reason given by the insurance company for the denial. This is typically found in the EOB. Identifying the denial reason allows you to address it directly in your appeal.

Grounds for Appeal: Provide a well-reasoned explanation for why the denial should be overturned. Your argument may include evidence of medical necessity, documentation of prior authorization, confirmation that the service is covered under the policy, or proof of accurate billing and coding. Explain clearly why the initial review was incorrect or incomplete.

Supporting Documentation: Attach all relevant supporting materials to reinforce your argument. These may include medical records, physician notes, diagnostic results, itemized bills, proof of prior authorization, and any additional documents. Ensure all attachments are legible, well-organized, and referenced appropriately within the letter.

Insurance Policy Coverage: If applicable, cite specific language from your insurance policy that supports your claim. Show how the services rendered align with the covered benefits and explain why the denial contradicts the terms of coverage.

Request for Reevaluation: State plainly that you are appealing the denial and respectfully request a full and impartial reevaluation of the claim. Reinforce your intent to resolve the issue professionally and efficiently.

Polite and Professional Tone: Use courteous and professional language throughout the letter. Avoid emotional language, blame, or accusations. Maintaining a respectful tone enhances your credibility and increases the likelihood of a favorable outcome.

Contact Information: Include your full contact information (phone number and email address) so that the insurance company can easily reach you for further communication or clarification.

Signature: Conclude the letter with your name and signature. If mailing a physical copy, use a handwritten signature. For digital submissions, a typed signature is acceptable.

Tips for Writing an Effective and Persuasive Appeal Letter

To enhance the effectiveness of your appeal, consider the following best practices:

- **Be Prompt**: Submit your appeal as soon as possible. Most insurance companies have strict deadlines for filing appeals.
- **Address the Right Recipient**: Direct your letter to the correct department or individual. If possible, find a name and title to personalize the correspondence.

- **Be Concise and Focused**: State the purpose of the letter early and stay focused on the core issues. Avoid adding unrelated or excessive details.
- **Include Specific Details**: Reference the patient's full name, claim number, date of service, and the specific reason for the denial.
- **Clearly State Your Argument**: Use facts, documentation, and logical reasoning to make your case. Refute the denial point-by-point.
- **Reference Your Policy**: If your appeal is based on policy coverage, quote the relevant section of the policy and explain how it applies.
- **Organize the Letter Well**: Use headings or bullet points to make the letter easy to follow.
- **Avoid Confrontation**: Advocate firmly but respectfully. An argumentative tone can undermine your case.
- **Demonstrate Medical Necessity**: If applicable, explain clearly why the treatment was medically necessary, using clinical terminology and evidence.
- **Appeal to Reason**: When appropriate, include a brief appeal to the reviewer's sense of fairness or patient care.
- **Proofread Carefully**: Errors in grammar or spelling can reduce your letter's effectiveness. A polished letter reflects professionalism.
- **Follow Instructions**: Comply with any guidelines or forms provided by the insurer.
- **Keep Copies**: Retain copies of the letter and all supporting documents for your records.

- **Be Persistent**: If you do not receive a response in a reasonable time, follow up. Consistent communication shows you are serious about resolving the issue.

Chapter Reflection and Implementation Notes

What New Insights Did I Gain?

(Use this space to reflect on key takeaways from this chapter.)

How Can I Apply These Principles in My Practice?

(Note actionable steps or ideas inspired by this chapter.)

Additional Notes

(Use the lines below for any further notes, ideas, or observations.)

CHAPTER 8
CONTACTING INSURANCE PLANS

Contacting insurance plans is a vital task for healthcare providers and patients alike. It helps clarify coverage, understand policy details, resolve claims, and address coverage issues. Following proper communication practices can streamline these interactions, reducing frustration and improving outcomes. Here are some guidelines for effectively contacting insurance plans.

Guidelines for Effectively Contacting Insurance Plans

Gather Information: Before contacting the insurance plan, gather all relevant information, including your insurance policy number, the name of the insured individual (if different from yours), the date of service or claim, and any relevant documentation related to your inquiry.

Check the Insurance Plan's Website: Many insurance plans provide comprehensive information, frequently asked questions (FAQs), and contact details on their official websites. Check the website first to see if your query can be addressed there.

Contact Customer Service: The customer service department is the primary point of contact for most insurance-related inquiries. Look for the customer service phone number or email address on the insurance card or website. Be prepared to verify your identity by providing your policy details.

Choose the Right Time: To avoid long wait times, try contacting the insurance company during non-peak hours. Many insurance companies offer extended hours, which may be less busy outside typical business hours.

Be Patient and Calm: When discussing insurance matters, remain patient and calm, even if the situation is frustrating. This will help you communicate effectively with the representative. Explain your query or concern clearly and avoid using aggressive or confrontational language.

Keep Notes: It is imperative to record the date, time, and name of the customer service representative with whom you spoke. This information is crucial if you need to follow up or escalate the matter.

Ask for a Reference or Case Number: If your inquiry requires further investigation or follow-up, ask for a reference or case number. This number will help you track the progress of your request.

Seek Clarification: If you do not understand an aspect of your policy or coverage, ask for clarification from the customer service representative. It is essential to understand your benefits and any limitations or exclusions.

Escalate If Necessary: If you encounter difficulties in resolving your issue through customer service, request to speak with a supervisor or escalate the matter to higher management. Insurance companies often have escalation procedures for unresolved issues.

Utilize Online Tools: Some insurance plans offer online portals to access your policy information, claim status, and other essential details. Explore these resources, as they can provide quick answers to common queries.

Be Mindful of HIPAA Privacy Rules: When discussing personal health information, ensure you are compliant with HIPAA privacy rules. Share sensitive information only with authorized personnel.

Follow Up: If your inquiry requires additional action or resolution, follow up as needed. Keep track of the status and any commitments made during previous communications.

Contact Information and Guidelines for Reaching Out to Insurance Companies

Contacting insurance companies is essential to managing insurance coverage, understanding policy details, resolving claim issues, and seeking assistance with various insurance-related matters. Whether you have questions about the policy, need to submit a claim, or want to appeal a denial, having accurate contact information and following guidelines for contacting insurance companies can streamline the process and ensure a better customer experience.

Finding Contact Information

Insurance Card: The first place to find contact information for an insurance company is on the insurance card. Typically, the card will display a customer service phone number, a website, and sometimes an email address.

Insurance Company Website: Visit the official website of the insurance company. They often provide a dedicated "Contact Us" or "Customer Service" section with various contact options, such as phone numbers, email addresses, and online chat support.

Policy Documents: Review the insurance policy documents, such as the policy handbook or welcome package. These documents may contain contact information for customer service, claims, and other relevant departments.

Mobile Apps: If your insurance company offers a mobile app, you can often find contact information within the app. Some apps also allow you to submit claims and access policy details directly.

Online Search: If you cannot find contact information using the methods above, conduct an online search by entering your insurance company's name and "customer service contact" or a similar query.

Guidelines for Reaching Out to Insurance Companies

Prepare Your Information: Before contacting the insurance company, gather all relevant information, including your policy number, claim details (if applicable), dates of service, and any documentation related to your inquiry.

Check Operating Hours: Many insurance companies have specific operating hours for their customer service departments. Make sure to call during their business hours to avoid delays in reaching a representative.

Choose the Right Communication Channel: Insurance companies offer various communication methods, including phone calls, emails, online chat, and social media. Choose the channel that best suits your needs.

Phone Calls

- **Be Patient:** Call volumes may be high, especially during peak hours, so be patient while waiting to speak with a representative.
- **Verify Your Identity:** Be prepared to provide identifying information, such as your name, policy number, and date of birth, to verify your identity.

Emails

- **Use a Clear Subject Line:** If you are contacting the insurance company via email, use a clear and concise subject line to indicate the purpose of your inquiry.
- **Provide Complete Information:** In your email, include all necessary details related to your inquiry to help the insurance company understand your situation.

Online Chat Support

- **Stay Online:** If you choose to use the online chat option, remain on the website until your inquiry is resolved or you are directed to the appropriate department.
- **Be Polite and Respectful:** Whether you communicate through phone calls, emails, or chat support, throughout the conversation, maintain a polite and respectful demeanor.

Other Guidelines

- **Be Specific and Concise:** Clearly state the reason for your inquiry or concern, and provide relevant details without unnecessary tangents or unrelated information.
- **Ask for Reference Numbers:** If your inquiry requires further follow-up or resolution, ask for a reference number or case ID to track the progress of your request.
- **Escalate If Necessary:** If you cannot resolve your issue with the initial customer service representative, request a meeting with a supervisor or escalate the situation to a higher management level.
- **Keep a Record:** Record all interactions with the insurance company, including dates, times, names of representatives, and any commitments or promises made.

Common Reasons to Contact Insurance Companies

- **Policy Inquiries:** For questions about the insurance policy, coverage details, benefits, and exclusions.
- **Claims Assistance:** For help with the status of a claim, to report a new claim, or to resolve issues with denied or underpaid claims.
- **Billing and Payments:** For inquiries about reimbursement payments, co-payments, deductibles, or billing statements.
- **Pre-Authorization:** To request pre-authorization for medical procedures or treatments that require prior approval from the insurer.
- **Network Providers:** To verify if a particular healthcare provider is in-network or out-of-network.
- **Coverage Questions:** To seek clarification on what medical services or treatments are covered under the insurance policy.
- **Policy Changes:** To update personal information, change the insurance policy, or add or delete dependents, patients must contact the healthcare plan.
- **Appeals and Disputes:** To initiate an appeal or dispute a claim denial or coverage decision.
- **Health Savings Accounts (HSAs) or Flexible Spending Accounts (FSAs):** For information on managing and using these accounts for eligible expenses.
- **Contacting Emergency Services:** Contact emergency services immediately by dialing your local emergency number (e.g., 911 in the United States). Insurance companies may have

separate emergency contact numbers for specific situations, such as international travel emergencies.

- **Dealing with Sensitive Information:** When discussing personal health information with insurance representatives, be cautious of the Health Insurance Portability and Accountability Act (HIPAA) privacy standards. Do not share sensitive information with anyone other than authorized personnel.

Tips for Effective Communication to Resolve Issues Promptly

Effective communication is crucial for resolving issues promptly and efficiently. Whether dealing with customer service representatives, colleagues, or any other party, employing the right communication strategies can lead to faster resolutions. Here are some tips for effective communication to help resolve issues promptly:

- **Be Clear and Concise:** Clearly articulate the issue you are facing. Avoid using jargon or unnecessary details that might confuse the listener. Focus on the key points to ensure a quick understanding of the problem.

- **Provide Relevant Information:** Share all pertinent information upfront, including dates, claim numbers, and any supporting documentation that can help the other person quickly grasp the context.

- **Active Listening:** When discussing the issue, pay attention to the representative's responses, questions, and advice to ensure you fully understand their perspective and concerns.

- **Stay Calm and Composed:** Even if the situation is frustrating, remaining calm helps you communicate more effectively and encourages a more positive outcome.
- **Use Polite and Respectful Language:** Being courteous goes a long way in resolving issues. Avoid using aggressive or accusatory language, as it can hinder progress in resolving the issue.
- **Choose the Right Communication Channel:** For urgent matters, consider calling; for less urgent inquiries, emails or online chat may be more appropriate.
- **Be Flexible and Open-Minded:** Be open to considering alternative solutions and compromises to resolve the issue.
- **Ask for Clarification:** If you do not understand something, do not hesitate to ask for clarification.
- **Confirm Understanding:** After discussing the issue, summarize the main points to ensure both parties are on the same page.
- **Set Clear Expectations:** Clearly communicate specific actions or follow-up steps and set realistic time frames for resolution.
- **Follow Up:** If the issue requires further investigation or resolution, follow up as agreed upon and provide any additional information requested.
- **Escalate Appropriately:** If the issue remains unresolved despite your efforts, inquire about the escalation process.
- **Document Communication:** Keep a record of all communication, including dates, times, names of individuals involved, and any agreements made.

- **Be Patient:** Some issues may take time to resolve, especially if they involve complex matters or multiple parties.
- **Express Gratitude:** Regardless of the outcome, express gratitude for the other person's time and effort. Showing appreciation fosters a positive relationship and leaves a lasting impression.

Chapter Reflection and Implementation Notes

What New Insights Did I Gain?

(Use this space to reflect on key takeaways from this chapter.)

How Can I Apply These Principles in My Practice?

(Note actionable steps or ideas inspired by this chapter.)

Additional Notes

(Use the lines below for any further notes, ideas, or observations.)

CHAPTER 9
POLICIES AND PROCEDURES

Policies and procedures are integral to any organized and efficient system, whether in a business, government agency, healthcare institution, or other organization. They serve as guiding principles and operational guidelines that help ensure consistency, compliance, and proper functioning. This chapter explores the role of policies and procedures, emphasizing their importance in achieving organizational goals, maintaining compliance, and enhancing efficiency.

Understanding Policies and Procedures

Policies: Policies are broad, overarching statements that reflect an organization's intentions, objectives, and principles. They set the tone for decision-making, outline acceptable behavior, and establish a framework for achieving specific goals. Policies often address vital areas such as ethics, human resources, safety, and quality assurance. They provide a foundation for the development of more detailed procedures.

Procedures: Procedures, on the other hand, are specific step-by-step instructions that detail how tasks should be performed. They provide a clear roadmap for executing activities consistently and efficiently. Procedures break down complex processes into manageable actions, making it easier for employees to follow established protocols.

Significance of Policies and Procedures

Consistency and Standardization: Policies and procedures ensure consistency in executing tasks. This consistency is crucial for maintaining product or service quality, meeting regulatory requirements, and minimizing errors.

Compliance: Well-defined policies and procedures help organizations adhere to laws, regulations, and industry standards. They provide a clear framework for mitigating legal risks and promoting ethical practices.

Efficiency and Productivity: By outlining the most effective and efficient task completion methods, procedures streamline processes and boost productivity. Employees can follow established steps, improving efficiency and productivity while reducing confusion and wasted time.

Training and Onboarding: Clear procedures act as essential tools for training new employees. They provide a structured approach to learning job responsibilities and integrating into the organization effectively.

Risk Management: Policies and procedures establish guidelines for mitigating risks, such as accidents, data breaches, or noncompliance with regulations, protecting both the organization and its stakeholders.

Communication: They facilitate consistent communication within the organization by clarifying expectations and guidelines, reducing misunderstandings, and aligning everyone with the organizational goals.

Decision-Making: Policies provide a framework for making informed and consistent decisions that align with the organization's values and objectives.

Examples of Policies and Procedures

- **Code of Conduct Policy:** This policy outlines expected behavior and ethical standards for employees. It addresses issues such as honesty, integrity, respect, and professionalism.
- **Employee Leave Policy:** Details the procedures for requesting and approving different types of employee leave, including vacation, sick leave, and parental leave.
- **Information Security Policy:** Outlines the guidelines for safeguarding sensitive information, including data protection, access controls, and cybersecurity practices.
- **Health and Safety Policy:** This policy outlines measures to ensure a safe working environment, including procedures for reporting accidents, using personal protective equipment, and responding to emergencies.
- **Procurement Policy:** Governs the acquisition of goods and services, specifying the steps for vendor selection, purchasing procedures, and budget considerations.
- **Performance Evaluation Procedure:** This procedure outlines the steps for conducting employee performance evaluations, including setting goals, providing feedback, and assessing performance.
- **Customer Service Procedure:** This procedure details the process for interacting with customers, handling inquiries, resolving complaints, and ensuring a positive customer experience.
- **Financial Reporting Policy:** Specifies precise and transparent protocols for financial reporting, including

documenting transactions, producing financial statements, and conducting audits.

- **IT Usage Procedure:** This procedure provides guidelines for using technology resources responsibly, including rules for software installation, internet usage, data backup, and cyber-security protocols.

Steps to Developing Effective Policies and Procedures

1. **Identify Needs:** Identify areas where policies and procedures are needed, considering compliance requirements, safety concerns, efficiency improvements, and other relevant factors.
2. **Research and Review:** Ensure that your policies and procedures are in line with the latest best practices, industry standards, and legal requirements through thorough research.
3. **Involve Stakeholders:** Collaborate with employees, managers, and legal experts to gather input, ensuring policies and procedures comprehensively cover relevant issues.
4. **Write Clearly:** Use simple, concise language to ensure that policies are easy to understand. Avoid jargon or overly technical terms to prevent confusion.
5. **Provide Examples:** Enhance clarity by providing real-world examples that demonstrate the application of the policies and procedures.
6. **Test and Revise:** Pilot policies and procedures in real-world scenarios before finalization. Revise based on feedback to ensure they are practical and effective.

7. **Training and Communication:** Provide thorough training to ensure employees understand new policies and procedures. Use multiple communication channels to reach all staff.

8. **Regular Review and Updates:** Regularly review policies to ensure they remain current with regulatory changes, industry trends, and organizational shifts.

Essential Office Policies and Procedures for Billing, Insurance, and Patient Interactions

Effective office policies and procedures related to billing, insurance, and patient interactions are crucial for maintaining effortless operations, ensuring accurate financial transactions, and providing exceptional patient care. Here, we'll cover some essential policies and procedures in these areas to help healthcare facilities and medical offices maintain professionalism, compliance, and patient satisfaction.

Billing Policies and Procedures

- **Clear Fee Schedule:** Maintain a comprehensive fee schedule that outlines the costs of various services and procedures. Ensure that this schedule is transparent and easily accessible to both staff and patients.

- **Verification of Insurance:** Implement a procedure for verifying patients' insurance coverage before their appointment. This can help prevent misunderstandings and ensure accurate billing.

- **Insurance Pre-Authorization Process:** Establish a process for obtaining preauthorization from insurance providers for specific procedures or treatments that require prior approval.

- **Patient Billing Statements:** Develop a policy for regularly generating and sending patient billing statements. Ensure that the statements are clear and easy to understand and provide detailed information about the services rendered.

- **Payment Plans:** Outline guidelines for setting up payment plans for patients who may need to pay their bills over time. Specify the terms, interest rates (if applicable), and payment schedule.

- **Collections Procedures:** Define steps to be taken for pursuing overdue payments, including sending reminders, working with collection agencies (if necessary), and the potential consequences of nonpayment.

- **Patient Financial Counseling:** Provide guidelines for offering financial counseling to patients who may have difficulty covering their medical expenses. Ensure that patients are informed about available assistance programs.

- **Medical Billing Coding:** Establish procedures for accurate medical coding to prevent errors and maximize insurance reimbursements.

Insurance Policies and Procedures

- **Insurance Verification:** Clearly outline the process for verifying patients' insurance coverage, including the required documentation and timing.

- **In-Network vs. Out-of-Network:** Educate staff on determining whether a patient's insurance covers specific healthcare providers or facilities.

- **Prior Authorization:** Detail the steps for obtaining prior authorization from insurance companies for specific treatments, tests, or procedures.
- **Claim Submission:** Provide guidelines for accurately preparing and submitting insurance claims to ensure timely reimbursement.
- **Appeals Process:** Develop a procedure for appealing denied insurance claims, including the necessary documentation and steps to take.
- **Coordination of Benefits:** Outline how to handle situations where a patient has multiple insurance plans, clarifying which one should be billed as the primary and secondary insurer.
- **Patient Education:** Develop policies for educating patients about their insurance coverage, including copays, deductibles, and coverage limitations.

Patient Interaction Policies and Procedures

- **Appointment Scheduling:** Establish efficient procedures for scheduling appointments, accommodating urgent cases, and handling cancellations.
- **Patient Check-In:** Define clear steps for verifying patient information, collecting forms, and ensuring insurance coverage at check-in.
- **Patient Privacy (HIPAA):** Implement a comprehensive policy to ensure patient privacy in compliance with the Health Insurance Portability and Accountability Act (HIPAA). Outline procedures for maintaining the confidentiality of patient information.

- **Informed Consent:** Detail the process for obtaining informed consent from patients before medical procedures or treatments.
- **Effective Communication:** Emphasize the importance of clear and respectful communication with patients, including active listening and addressing patient concerns.
- **Patient Complaints and Grievances:** Develop a formal procedure for handling and documenting patient complaints, ensuring prompt resolution.
- **Cultural Sensitivity:** Provide guidelines for interacting with diverse patient populations to ensure respect and understanding.
- **Patient Discharge:** Outline the process for patient discharge, including providing necessary instructions, medications, and follow-up appointments.

Emphasizing Compliance with Legal and Ethical Standards

Emphasizing compliance with legal and ethical standards is paramount in all aspects of healthcare, including billing, insurance, and patient interactions. Adhering to these standards not only ensures the integrity of your practice but also maintains trust with patients and upholds the reputation of the healthcare industry as a whole. Here's how to place a strong emphasis on compliance within these areas:

Billing Policies and Procedures

- **Accuracy and Transparency:** Stress the importance of accurately documenting and transparently communicating all financial transactions. Ensure that bills and statements reflect the actual services provided and costs incurred.

- **Upcoding and Unbundling:** Prohibit practices like upcoding (billing for a higher level of service than performed) and unbundling (billing separately for components billed as a single service).
- **Anti-Kickback and Stark Laws:** Educate staff about the Anti-Kickback Statute and Stark Law, which prohibit offering, soliciting, or accepting incentives for referrals or services. Emphasize the need to avoid any arrangements that may violate these laws.
- **False Claims Act:** Communicate the consequences of submitting false claims to government healthcare programs and stress the importance of accuracy in claims submissions.
- **Prompt Payment Rules:** Ensure that prompt payment rules are followed and emphasize the importance of timely reimbursements to prevent delays.

Insurance Policies and Procedures

- **Fraud Prevention:** Clearly state the zero-tolerance policy for insurance fraud, including providing false information, misrepresenting services, or inflating claims.
- **Ethical Billing Practices:** Emphasize that all billing practices should adhere to ethical standards, ensuring that services billed are accurately documented and supported by appropriate medical records.
- **In-Network Compliance:** Instruct staff to diligently verify and confirm in-network status to avoid billing out-of-network rates when unnecessary.

- **Patient Privacy and HIPAA:** Reiterate the significance of patient privacy and the consequences of violating the Health Insurance Portability and Accountability Act (HIPAA). Stress the importance of safeguarding patient information and obtaining proper consent.

Patient Interaction Policies and Procedures

- **Informed Consent:** Emphasize the ethical obligation to obtain informed consent from patients before conducting any procedures, ensuring they are well aware of the risks, benefits, and alternatives.

- **Cultural Competence:** Emphasize the importance of cultural competence in patient interactions. Highlight the ethical obligation to provide respectful and unbiased care regardless of a patient's background.

- **Patient Dignity and Respect:** Communicate the ethical imperative of treating all patients with dignity, respect, and compassion, regardless of their condition or circumstances.

- **Confidentiality and Trust:** Reinforce the significance of maintaining patient confidentiality. Remind staff that breach of patient trust through unauthorized information sharing is unethical and illegal.

- **Reporting Concerns:** Establish clear procedures for reporting any suspected legal or ethical violations. Encourage a culture where staff feel comfortable raising concerns without fear of reprisal.

Continuous Training and Monitoring

- **Regular Training:** Provide ongoing legal and ethical compliance training, reinforcing the importance of adhering to established policies and procedures.
- **Audits and Monitoring:** Conduct regular audits to assess adherence to billing, insurance, and patient interaction policies. Address any discrepancies promptly and use these opportunities to enhance compliance.
- **Open Communication:** Foster an environment where staff members feel comfortable asking questions, seeking clarifications, and reporting potential compliance issues.
- **Accountability:** Hold all employees accountable for adhering to the law and ethical standards. Establish consequences for violations and consistently apply them.

Chapter Reflection and Implementation Notes

What New Insights Did I Gain?

(Use this space to reflect on key takeaways from this chapter.)

How Can I Apply These Principles in My Practice?

(Note actionable steps or ideas inspired by this chapter.)

Additional Notes

(Use the lines below for any further notes, ideas, or observations.)

CHAPTER 10: ACTION PLAN

To incorporate best practices, ensure compliance, and raise the standard of medical treatment in billing, insurance, and patient relations, it is essential to develop and implement an effective action plan. Here's a step-by-step action plan that outlines steps to achieve these goals:

Step 1: Assessment and Gap Analysis

Conduct a Comprehensive Assessment: Evaluate your billing, insurance, and patient interaction processes. Identify areas of improvement, potential risks, and compliance gaps.

Review Legal and Ethical Standards: Ensure a clear understanding of legal and ethical requirements in healthcare billing, insurance, and patient interactions.

Benchmark Best Practices: Research and benchmark industry best practices in billing, insurance, and patient care. Identify leading organizations and learn from their successful strategies.

Step 2: Policy and Procedure Development

Form a Cross-Functional Team: Establish a team comprising billing specialists, insurance coordinators, patient service representatives, legal advisors, and healthcare administrators.

Review and Revise Policies: Collaboratively review existing policies and procedures in billing, insurance, and patient interactions. Revise and align them with best practices and legal requirements.

Draft New Policies: Develop new policies and procedures where needed, encompassing accurate coding, ethical billing, insurance verification, and patient-centered interactions.

Legal and Ethical Compliance: Incorporate language in policies and procedures that explicitly emphasize compliance with legal and ethical standards.

Step 3: Staff Training and Education

Develop Training Modules: Create comprehensive training modules on billing accuracy, insurance processes, patient interactions, and compliance with legal and ethical standards.

Training Sessions: Conduct interactive training sessions for staff, emphasizing the importance of best practices and the role of compliance in healthcare operations.

Continuous Education: Establish an ongoing education program to keep staff informed about industry changes, new regulations, and emerging best practices.

Step 4: Implementation and Integration

Roll Out New Policies: Communicate and introduce the updated policies and procedures to all staff members. Provide clear instructions on their implementation.

Role-Specific Training: Tailor training sessions to specific roles within billing, insurance, and patient interactions to address role-specific challenges.

Integration with EHR and Software: Collaborate with IT teams to integrate best practices into electronic health record (EHR) systems and billing software for seamless execution.

Step 5: Monitoring and Auditing

Establish Auditing Procedures: Develop a system for regular internal audits to assess adherence to best practices and identify areas for improvement.

Audit Frequency: Set a schedule for audits, ensuring they occur regularly to monitor ongoing compliance.

Feedback and Reporting: Implement a feedback mechanism where staff can report potential compliance issues, errors, or suggestions for process enhancement.

Step 6: Continuous Improvement

Form Quality Improvement Teams: Form cross-functional quality improvement teams focused on billing, insurance, and patient interactions.

Regular Review Meetings: Conduct regular review meetings to discuss audit findings, share insights, and brainstorm innovative solutions.

Implement Enhancements: Use feedback, audit results, and team discussions to implement process enhancements and address identified gaps.

Step 7: Communication and Transparency

Patient Communication: Communicate changes and improvements in billing, insurance, and patient interactions to patients through informative materials and clear explanations.

Internal Communication: Foster a culture of open communication within the organization, encouraging staff to share concerns, suggestions, and success stories.

Step 8: Recognition and Incentives

Recognition Programs: Introduce recognition programs to acknowledge and celebrate staff members who consistently adhere to best practices and contribute to positive outcomes.

Incentive Structures: Consider implementing incentive structures that reward staff for achieving compliance goals and delivering exceptional patient experiences.

Step 9: Ongoing Evaluation

Regular Assessment: Continuously assess the effectiveness of implemented best practices, policies, and procedures through audits, patient feedback, and performance metrics.

Adaptation and Improvement: Based on evaluations, adapt and refine your action plan to address changing industry trends, regulations, and organizational needs.

Key Takeaways from the Guide

The guide provides a comprehensive overview of implementing best practices in healthcare settings, specifically focusing on billing, insurance, and patient interactions. Here are the key takeaways:

Importance of Best Practices: Best practices are proven methods and approaches that enhance efficiency, compliance, and patient satisfaction. They are essential for maintaining high-quality healthcare services and upholding legal and ethical standards.

Billing Policies and Procedures

- **Accurate Coding and Documentation:** Use standardized codes and ensure clear documentation to prevent errors and ensure proper reimbursement.
- **Transparency and Compliance:** Maintain a transparent fee schedule, verify insurance, and adhere to legal billing guidelines.
- **Prevent Fraud:** Prohibit unethical practices like upcoding and unbundling, and emphasize accurate billing to prevent fraud.

Insurance Policies and Procedures

- **Verification and Authorization:** Establish protocols for verifying insurance coverage and obtaining preauthorization for procedures.
- **Accurate Claims Submission:** Implement procedures for submitting accurate and timely insurance claims to ensure reimbursement.
- **Ethical Billing:** Stress ethical billing practices, proper coding, and compliance with regulations to prevent errors and fraud.

Patient Interactions Policies and Procedures

- **Patient-Centered Care:** Prioritize patient needs, communication, and respect to provide compassionate and personalized care.
- **Informed Consent:** Obtain informed consent for procedures, ensuring patients understand risks, benefits, and alternatives.

- **Cultural Sensitivity:** Train staff in cultural competence to provide inclusive and respectful care to diverse patient populations.

Compliance with Legal and Ethical Standards

- **HIPAA and Privacy:** Emphasize patient privacy and compliance with HIPAA regulations to safeguard patient information.
- **Anti-Fraud Laws:** Educate staff about anti-kickback laws, Stark Law, and the False Claims Act to prevent fraudulent activities.
- **Code of Conduct:** Enforce a robust code of conduct that upholds ethical behavior and integrity in all interactions.

Implementation of Best Practices

- **Assess Current Practices:** Conduct a thorough assessment to identify gaps and areas for improvement in billing, insurance, and patient interactions.
- **Develop Policies:** Formulate clear and comprehensive policies and procedures aligned with best practices and legal requirements.
- **Prevent Fraud:** Prohibit unethical practices like upcoding and unbundling, and emphasize accurate billing to prevent fraud.

Monitoring and Continuous Improvement

- **Internal Audits:** Establish a system for regular internal audits to monitor adherence to best practices and identify opportunities for enhancement.
- **Quality Improvement Teams:** Form cross-functional teams to address specific aspects of billing, insurance, and patient interactions.
- **Ongoing Evaluation:** Continuously assess the effectiveness of implemented practices and make necessary adaptations based on feedback and data.

Communication and Transparency

- **Patient Education:** Provide patients with clear information about billing, insurance, and procedures to promote transparency and informed decision-making.
- **Internal Communication:** Foster open communication within the organization to encourage reporting of concerns and suggestions.

Recognition and Incentives

- **Staff Recognition:** Implement programs to recognize and reward staff members who consistently adhere to best practices and contribute to positive outcomes.
- **Incentive Structures:** Consider introducing incentives that motivate staff to achieve compliance goals and deliver exceptional patient experiences.

Continuous Commitment

Emphasize that integrating best practices is an ongoing commitment to delivering high-quality healthcare services, ensuring compliance, and fostering a culture of continuous improvement.

An Action Plan for Implementing the Guidelines Effectively

This action plan focuses on incorporating best practices and fostering a culture of continuous improvement in healthcare billing, insurance processes, and patient interactions.

Phase 1: Preparation and Assessment

Form an Implementation Team: Create a cross-functional team comprising billing specialists, insurance coordinators, patient service representatives, compliance officers, legal advisors, and healthcare administrators.

Orientation and Training: Conduct an orientation session for the implementation team to ensure everyone understands the implementation process's purpose, goals, and expected outcomes.

Assessment and Gap Analysis: Collaboratively assess current billing, insurance, and patient interaction practices. Identify areas of improvement, compliance gaps, and opportunities for enhancing patient experiences.

Phase 2: Policy and Procedure Development

Review and Revise Policies: Evaluate existing policies and procedures in billing, insurance, and patient interactions. Revise them to align with best practices and legal and ethical standards.

Draft New Policies: Draft new policies and procedures where gaps exist, incorporating recommendations from industry best practices and legal requirements.

Legal and Ethical Compliance Emphasis: Infuse policies with explicit language emphasizing compliance with legal regulations, ethical standards, and patient privacy rights.

Phase 3: Training and Education

Training Material Creation: Develop comprehensive training modules and materials on accurate billing, insurance processes, patient-centered interactions, ethical conduct, and compliance.

Training Sessions: Conduct interactive training sessions for all relevant staff members, including billing teams, insurance coordinators, patient service representatives, and healthcare providers.

Role-Specific Training: Tailor training sessions to specific roles within billing, insurance, and patient interactions to address role-specific challenges and responsibilities.

Phase 4: Implementation and Integration

Policy Rollout: Communicate the updated policies and procedures to all staff members through clear communication channels, highlighting their importance and relevance.

Integration with Systems: Collaborate with the IT department to integrate best practices into electronic health record (EHR) systems, billing software, and communication tools.

Trial Period and Feedback Collection: Implement the new policies on a trial basis. Gather feedback from staff to identify any practical challenges or areas needing further clarification.

Phase 5: Monitoring and Auditing

Audit Framework Development: Establish a systematic framework for conducting regular internal audits to evaluate adherence to best practices and compliance standards.

Audit Schedule: Set a schedule for conducting audits, ensuring they occur consistently (e.g., quarterly) to monitor ongoing compliance.

Feedback Mechanism: Create a reporting mechanism for staff to provide feedback on compliance, errors, process bottlenecks, and suggestions for improvement.

Phase 6: Continuous Improvement

Quality Improvement Teams: Form cross-functional quality improvement teams focused on billing, insurance, and patient interactions, such as accuracy, efficiency, and patient satisfaction.

Regular Review Meetings: Organize periodic review meetings with the implementation and quality improvement teams to discuss audit findings, share insights, and brainstorm solutions.

Process Enhancement: Based on feedback, audit results, and team discussions, identify areas for process enhancement and implement changes that align with best practices.

Phase 7: Communication and Transparency

Patient Communication: Develop patient-friendly materials that clearly explain billing, insurance, and procedures. Ensure patients are informed about their rights, options, and costs.

Internal Communication Channels: Foster a culture of open communication within the organization, encouraging staff to share concerns, suggestions, and success stories.

Phase 8: Recognition and Incentives

Recognition Programs: Establish programs that acknowledge and celebrate staff members who consistently adhere to best practices and contribute to positive outcomes.

Incentive Structures: Consider introducing incentives that motivate staff to achieve compliance goals, deliver exceptional patient experiences, and actively engage in process improvement.

Phase 9: Ongoing Evaluation

Regular Assessment: Continuously assess the effectiveness of implemented best practices, policies, and procedures through audits, patient feedback, and performance metrics.

Adaptation and Refinement: Based on evaluations, adapt and refine the implementation plan to address changing industry trends, regulations, and organizational needs.

Phase 10: Recognition and Incentives

Cultivate a Culture of Excellence: Instill a culture of continuous improvement, ethical conduct, and patient-centered care across all levels of the organization.

Ongoing Training and Development: Sustain ongoing training, development, and awareness campaigns to keep staff engaged and informed about best practices, regulatory changes, and ethical guidelines.

Leadership Support and Communication: Ensure leadership actively supports the implementation efforts, regularly communicates progress, and reinforces the importance of compliance.

Resources for Continuous Learning and Improvement

Continuous learning and improvement are essential in healthcare to stay updated with industry advancements, regulations, and best practices. Here's a list of valuable resources that healthcare professionals and organizations can utilize for ongoing education and enhancement:

Online Courses and Training Platforms

- **Coursera:** Offers a wide range of healthcare-related courses, including medical coding, healthcare management, patient communication, and compliance.

  Website: coursera.org

- **edX:** Provides healthcare courses from top universities and institutions worldwide, covering healthcare innovation, patient safety, and healthcare technology.

  Website: edx.org

- **LinkedIn Learning:** Offers courses on healthcare management, compliance, leadership, and soft skills like communication and cultural competence.

  Website: linkedin.com/learning

- **American Health Information Management Association (AHIMA):** Offers online courses and webinars on medical coding, health information management, and healthcare compliance.

  Website: ahima.org

Professional Associations and Organizations

- **American Medical Association (AMA):** Provides resources on medical billing and coding, healthcare management, and regulatory updates.

  Website: ama-assn.org

- **Healthcare Financial Management Association (HFMA):** Focuses on healthcare financial management, offering education, webinars, and resources on revenue cycle management.

  Website: hfma.org

- **American Association of Healthcare Administrative Management (AAHAM):** Provides resources and events related to healthcare administrative and revenue cycle management.

  Website: aaham.org

Regulatory and Compliance Resources

- **Centers for Medicare and Medicaid Services (CMS):** Offers guidance, updates, and educational resources on healthcare billing, coding, and compliance.

  Website: cms.gov

- **Office of Inspector General (OIG):** Provides compliance resources, guidelines, and insights to prevent fraud and abuse in healthcare.

  Website: oig.hhs.gov

- **HealthIT.gov:** Offers information on healthcare technology, electronic health records (EHR), and meaningful use compliance.

  Website: healthit.gov

Books and Publications

- *The Healthcare Quality Book: Vision, Strategy, and Tools* by David Nash

  A comprehensive guide to improving healthcare quality and patient outcomes.

- *Lean Hospitals: Enhancing Patient Safety, Quality, and Staff Engagement* by Mark Graban

  Explains how lean principles can enhance healthcare processes.

- *The Patient Will See You Now: The Future of Medicine Is in Your Hands* by Eric Topol

Explores the impact of technology on patient interactions and healthcare delivery.

Conferences and Events

- **Healthcare Conferences:** Attend industry-specific conferences and events on medical billing, coding, compliance, and healthcare management.
- **Local Workshops:** Look for regional workshops, seminars, and webinars hosted by healthcare organizations, universities, and professional associations.

Industry Journals and Magazines

- **The Journal of the American Medical Association (JAMA):** Publishes research papers, analyses, and news on developments in medicine and healthcare.

  Website: jamanetwork.com

- **Healthcare Financial Management:** A publication by HFMA covering revenue cycle management, financial strategies, and industry trends.

  Website: hfma.org/industry-insight

Online Forums and Communities

- **Healthcare Forums and Communities:** Participate in online forums and groups related to medical billing, coding, healthcare compliance, and patient interactions. These platforms provide peer-to-peer support and shared insights.

Chapter Reflection and Implementation Notes

What New Insights Did I Gain?

(Use this space to reflect on key takeaways from this chapter.)

How Can I Apply These Principles in My Practice?

(Note actionable steps or ideas inspired by this chapter.)

Additional Notes

(Use the lines below for any further notes, ideas, or observations.)

CHAPTER 11
INADEQUATE FOLLOW-UP ON CLAIMS

In the realm of insurance and financial sectors, claim determination stands as a critical process, serving as the nexus between policyholders and insurers. It embodies the pivotal moment where the promise of coverage meets the reality of reimbursement or compensation. However, the efficiency and effectiveness of this process heavily rely on meticulous follow-up procedures. Despite its paramount importance, the lack of proper follow-up on claim determination status presents a significant challenge within the industry.

This introduction delves into the multifaceted dimensions of the issue, exploring its implications, causes, and potential remedies. From delayed reimbursements to strained customer relations, the consequences of inadequate follow-up reverberate throughout the insurance landscape, impacting stakeholders at every level. Moreover, underlying factors such as resource constraints, technological limitations, and organizational inefficiencies often exacerbate this problem, warranting a comprehensive examination.

At its core, the failure to promptly follow up on claim determination status not only undermines the trust between insurers and policyholders but also engenders operational inefficiencies and financial ramifications. As such, addressing this challenge demands proactive strategies that amalgamate technological innovations, streamlined processes, and a customer-centric ethos.

Purpose of the Guide

This guide seeks to explore the following key aspects of inadequate follow-up on claims:

- **Importance of Follow-Up:** We will highlight the necessity of effective follow-up in the claim determination process, emphasizing its role in ensuring transparency, improving customer relations, and maintaining operational efficiency.
- **Challenges and Pitfalls:** Common challenges like delayed payments, customer dissatisfaction, and regulatory issues will be examined to better understand the consequences of ineffective follow-up.
- **Best Practices and Strategies:** This section will provide actionable solutions to improve follow-up procedures, from leveraging technology to implementing clear communication protocols.
- **Stakeholder Perspectives:** We will examine the viewpoints of insurers, policyholders, and regulators on follow-up practices, offering insights into how each group's expectations shape follow-up strategies.
- **Case Studies and Examples:** Real-world examples will illustrate how effective follow-up practices can positively impact claim outcomes.
- **Regulatory Considerations:** The legal framework governing the insurance industry will be discussed, particularly how regulations influence follow-up requirements and the penalties for noncompliance.

Importance of Effective Claims Follow-Up

The importance of effective follow-up in the claims process cannot be overstated. A lack of timely follow-up can undermine relationships with policyholders, create operational bottlenecks, and lead to compliance issues. Here's why effective follow-up is essential:

- **Customer Satisfaction:** Timely and proactive follow-up on claims demonstrates a commitment to customer service. It reassures policyholders that their claims are being processed, fostering trust and satisfaction with the insurance company. Conversely, a lack of follow-up can lead to frustration and dissatisfaction among policyholders.
- **Transparency and Trust:** Effective follow-up practices promote transparency in the claims process. By keeping policyholders informed about the status of their claims and any necessary documentation or actions required, insurers build trust and credibility. This transparency is essential for maintaining positive relationships with policyholders.
- **Faster Resolution:** Follow-up ensures that claims move through the processing pipeline efficiently. By identifying and addressing any issues or delays promptly, insurers can expedite claim resolution, minimizing disruptions for policyholders and reducing the time and resources required for claims processing.
- **Risk Mitigation:** Timely follow-up helps insurers identify potential issues or discrepancies early in the claims process. By addressing these issues promptly, insurers can mitigate the risk of fraud, errors, or misunderstandings, ultimately protecting their bottom line and preserving the integrity of the claims process.

- **Compliance and Regulatory Requirements:** Many jurisdictions have strict regulations governing claims handling and communication with policyholders. Effective follow-up practices help insurers remain compliant with these regulations, avoiding potential fines, penalties, or legal disputes that could arise from noncompliance.
- **Enhanced Reputation:** A reputation for efficient and responsive claims handling can be a significant competitive advantage for insurers. Positive word-of-mouth from satisfied policyholders can attract new customers and help retain existing ones. At the same time, negative experiences resulting from poor follow-up can damage an insurer's reputation and brand image.
- **Operational Efficiency:** By streamlining follow-up procedures and leveraging automation and technology solutions, insurers can improve the efficiency of their claims processing operations. This not only reduces administrative burdens and costs but also allows insurers to reallocate resources to other areas of the business where they can add more value.

Challenges and Pitfalls of Inadequate Follow-Up

Several challenges arise from inadequate follow-up on claims, including:

- **Delayed Payments:** Without timely follow-up, claims may take longer to process, leading to delayed reimbursements for policyholders. This can cause financial strain for both customers and insurers.
- **Customer Dissatisfaction:** Policyholders often become frustrated when they feel uninformed or neglected during the

claims process. A lack of follow-up communication can lead to lost trust and, ultimately, a damaged relationship with the insurer.

- **Compliance Issues:** Regulatory bodies impose timelines and communication requirements that must be met during the claims process. Failure to follow up in a timely manner can result in noncompliance, exposing the insurer to legal repercussions.

- **Increased Operational Costs:** When claims are not followed up on efficiently, it can lead to increased administrative costs, as insurers must dedicate more resources to track and resolve backlogged or delayed claims.

Best Practices and Strategies for Effective Claims Follow-Up

To avoid these pitfalls, insurers can adopt several best practices and strategies for improving follow-up procedures:

Leverage Technology Solutions: Implement claims management software that automates follow-up reminders and sends updates to policyholders at critical stages of the claims process. Automation reduces the risk of human error and ensures that no claim is left unattended.

Establish Clear Communication Protocols: Create standardized communication protocols that outline when and how follow-up should be conducted. For example, insurers could establish rules requiring follow-up at specific intervals, such as after claim submission, during the investigation phase, and before final determination.

Use Multiple Communication Channels: Offer multiple communication channels, such as phone, email, online portals, and even SMS, to keep policyholders informed. A multichannel approach accommodates different customer preferences and improves overall engagement.

Designate a Claims Follow-Up Team: Assign a dedicated team or individuals responsible for monitoring the status of claims and ensuring timely follow-up. By focusing solely on follow-up tasks, this team can prevent delays and keep claims moving efficiently through the pipeline.

Implement Key Performance Indicators (KPIs): Establish KPIs to monitor the effectiveness of claims follow-up processes. Metrics such as average follow-up time, claim processing times, and customer satisfaction scores can help insurers identify areas needing improvement.

Stakeholder Perspectives on Follow-Up

Understanding the needs and expectations of various stakeholders is essential for improving follow-up practices. Each group brings its own priorities to the claims process:

- **Insurers:** Insurers prioritize operational efficiency, regulatory compliance, and customer retention. They aim to minimize delays and maintain a positive reputation by resolving claims promptly.
- **Policyholders:** Policyholders expect timely updates, transparent communication, and fair handling of their claims. They want assurance that their claim is being processed fairly and efficiently, with minimal inconvenience.

- **Regulators:** Regulatory bodies impose strict guidelines on how claims should be processed, including timelines for follow-up. Regulators prioritize compliance to ensure fair treatment of policyholders and uphold industry standards.

Case Studies and Examples

Real-world examples provide valuable insights into how effective follow-up practices can positively impact claims outcomes. For example:

- **Case Study 1: Automating Claims Follow-Up**

  A leading insurance company implemented an automated follow-up system that sent claim status updates to policyholders at key stages. This reduced customer inquiries by 30 percent, improved satisfaction scores, and expedited claim resolutions by 15 percent.

- **Case Study 2: Dedicated Claims Support Team**

  Another insurer created a dedicated follow-up team responsible for tracking claims and initiating regular contact with policyholders. As a result, the company experienced a 20 percent decrease in claim processing times and a significant improvement in customer satisfaction.

Regulatory Considerations

The regulatory framework governing the insurance industry requires insurers to adhere to strict guidelines regarding claims processing and communication. Key regulations to keep in mind include:

- **Timeliness:** Insurers must comply with legally mandated timelines for responding to claims and providing updates to policyholders.
- **Fair Communication:** Regulations often require insurers to communicate clearly with policyholders, ensuring transparency throughout the claims process.
- **Documentation:** Insurers must maintain detailed records of all follow-up communications and actions taken during the claims process to demonstrate compliance during audits or legal inquiries.

Chapter Reflection and Implementation Notes

What New Insights Did I Gain?

(Use this space to reflect on key takeaways from this chapter.)

How Can I Apply These Principles in My Practice?

(Note actionable steps or ideas inspired by this chapter.)

Additional Notes

(Use the lines below for any further notes, ideas, or observations.)

CHAPTER 12
UNDERSTANDING THE CLAIMS PROCESS

The claims process in healthcare insurance is a critical component of the healthcare system. It involves several steps that ensure healthcare providers are reimbursed for services rendered to patients. Understanding this process is essential for both healthcare providers and patients to navigate the complexities of healthcare billing and insurance coverage.

The Steps in the Claims Process

1. **Patient Registration and Insurance Verification:** The process begins when a patient registers at a healthcare facility. During registration, the office staff collects and verifies the patient's insurance information, ensuring that the patient's insurance plan is active and covers the services they will receive. Verification of insurance coverage is crucial to ensure that the patient's plan covers the proposed medical services, reducing the risk of claim denials.

2. **Service Documentation:** After the patient receives medical services, healthcare providers document all the details of the visit, including diagnoses, treatments, and procedures performed. Accurate and detailed documentation is crucial as it forms the basis of the insurance claim.

3. **Coding:** Medical coders translate the documented services into standardized codes (ICD-10 for diagnoses and CPT for procedures). These codes are essential for the insurance companies to understand what services were provided and for billing purposes.

4. **Claim Submission:** Once the services are documented and coded, the healthcare provider submits the claim to the patient's insurance company. This claim includes the coded information, patient details, and a summary of services provided. Claims can be submitted electronically or via paper forms, though electronic submission is more common and efficient.

5. **Insurance Review:** Upon receiving the claim, the insurance company reviews it to ensure that the services are covered under the patient's insurance plan. This review process checks for accuracy, medical necessity, and adherence to the policy terms.

6. **Claim Adjudication:** The insurance company adjudicates the claim, determining the amount payable based on the patient's coverage and the terms of the insurance policy. They may approve, deny, or adjust the claim amount. They may request additional information or documentation if required.

7. **Payment or Denial and Explanation of Benefits (EOB):** After adjudication, the insurance company either approves the claim for payment or denies it. Approved claims result in reimbursement to the healthcare provider according to the insurance policy terms. Denied claims come with explanations, detailing the reasons for denial, such as coding errors, incomplete information, or noncovered services.

   When the claim is approved, the insurance company issues a payment to the healthcare provider and sends an Explanation of Benefits (EOB) to the patient. The EOB outlines what services were covered, the amount paid, and any patient responsibilities like copays or deductibles.

8. **Appeals and Resubmissions Process:** If a claim is denied or underpaid, healthcare providers can appeal the decision. The appeals process involves submitting additional documentation or correcting errors in the original claim to justify the necessity and coverage of the services provided. Resubmitting the claim after addressing the denial reasons is a crucial step to ensure payment.

9. **Payment Posting and Reconciliation:** Once payments are received, they are posted to the patient's account. Reconciliation involves ensuring that the payment matches the expected reimbursement and resolving any discrepancies.

10. **Patient Billing and Follow-Up:** Any remaining balance after insurance payment is billed to the patient. Providers must ensure clear communication with patients about their financial responsibilities and follow up on outstanding payments.

Importance of Understanding the Claims Process

For healthcare providers, understanding the claims process is essential for maintaining financial stability and ensuring timely reimbursement. Efficient claims management reduces denied claims, minimizes administrative costs, and improves cash flow.

Providers who thoroughly understand the intricacies of the insurance process can better advise patients about their coverage and potential out-of-pocket costs, which can significantly enhance patient satisfaction and trust.

Key Terminology: Submission, Adjudication, Denials

Submission: Submission refers to the process of sending a healthcare claim to the insurance company for review and payment. This step occurs after the healthcare provider has documented the patient's diagnosis and the services rendered, translated these into standardized medical codes, and gathered all necessary information.

Claims can be submitted electronically or on paper, although electronic submission is more prevalent due to its efficiency and speed. Accurate and complete submission is crucial to avoid delays or rejections. The claim must include patient demographics, provider details, dates of service, diagnosis codes (ICD-10), and procedure codes (CPT).

Adjudication: Adjudication is the process by which the insurance company reviews and processes the submitted claim. During adjudication, the insurer evaluates several factors: the accuracy of the information provided, the patient's eligibility, the medical necessity of the services, and the coverage under the patient's insurance policy.

This process determines whether the claim will be paid, partially paid, or denied. Adjudication involves checks for policy limits, coordination of benefits (if the patient has multiple insurances), and verification against any preauthorizations or referrals required for the services. The insurer may request additional documentation if there are discrepancies or insufficient information.

Denials: Denials occur when an insurance company refuses to pay a claim, either partially or entirely. Common reasons for denials include coding errors, incomplete or inaccurate information, services not covered by the patient's insurance plan, lack of medical necessity, or failure to obtain preauthorization.

When a claim is denied, the provider receives an Explanation of Benefits (EOB) or a denial letter detailing the reason for the denial. Providers can address the issues cited in the denial and resubmit the claim or file an appeal to contest the decision. Effective management of denials is crucial to maintain revenue flow and ensure that services are appropriately reimbursed.

Common Reasons for Claims Denials

Understanding common reasons for claims denials can help healthcare providers take proactive steps to reduce their occurrence and ensure reimbursement processes. Here are some of the most prevalent reasons for claims denials:

- **Incomplete or Inaccurate Information:** Claims that lack essential details or contain errors are frequently denied. This includes incorrect patient information, missing provider details, inaccurate service dates, or erroneous medical codes. Even minor mistakes in data entry can lead to denials. Ensuring that all required fields are accurately completed before submission is crucial.

- **Incorrect or Inconsistent Coding:** Medical coding errors are a leading cause of claims denials. These can include using outdated codes, mismatched diagnosis and procedure codes, or incorrect modifiers. Proper training in the latest ICD-10 and CPT codes and employing certified medical coders can significantly reduce these errors. Consistent internal audits can also help identify and correct coding discrepancies.

- **Lack of Medical Necessity:** Insurance companies often deny claims if they determine that the provided services were not medically necessary. To avoid this, healthcare providers must thoroughly document the patient's medical condition and justify the necessity of the treatments or procedures. Including comprehensive clinical notes and supporting documentation can strengthen the claim.

- **Preauthorization or Referral Issues:** Many insurance plans require preauthorization or referrals for certain services. Claims for these services will be denied if the necessary preauthorization was not obtained or if the referral is missing or incorrect. Establishing a robust preauthorization process and verifying referral requirements can prevent these denials.

- **Eligibility and Coverage Problems:** Claims can be denied if the patient's insurance coverage is inactive, the plan does not cover the service, or the patient has exceeded benefit limits. Verifying patient eligibility and benefits before providing services can mitigate these issues. Regularly updating insurance information and conducting preservice eligibility checks are vital steps.

- **Timely Filing Issues:** Insurance companies have specific deadlines for submitting claims. Claims submitted after the deadline are often denied. Healthcare providers must be aware of and adhere to these timelines to avoid denials. Implementing an efficient claims submission process and tracking system can ensure timely filing.

- **Coordination of Benefits (COB) Conflicts:** When a patient has multiple insurance plans, coordination of benefits ensures that the correct insurer is billed first. Failure to follow COB rules can result in denials. Accurate documentation of the primary and secondary insurance details and proper billing sequencing are essential to avoid COB-related denials.

- **Duplicate Claims:** Submitting the same claim multiple times, whether by mistake or due to system errors, can lead to denials. Establishing clear procedures for tracking submitted claims and using reliable billing software can help prevent duplicate claims.

Chapter Reflection and Implementation Notes

What New Insights Did I Gain?

(Use this space to reflect on key takeaways from this chapter.)

How Can I Apply These Principles in My Practice?

(Note actionable steps or ideas inspired by this chapter.)

Additional Notes

(Use the lines below for any further notes, ideas, or observations.)

CHAPTER 13
TEAM ROLES AND RESPONSIBILITIES

Effective teamwork hinges upon clearly defined roles and responsibilities that are aligned with the overall objectives of the team and the organization as a whole. Each team member brings unique skills, expertise, and perspectives to the table, and understanding their roles and responsibilities is essential for maximizing productivity, fostering collaboration, and achieving success. Here's a closer look at team roles and responsibilities.

Key Team Roles and Responsibilities

Leadership: The leadership role within a team is responsible for providing direction, guidance, and support to team members. Leaders set the vision and goals for the team, facilitate communication and decision-making, and ensure that everyone is working toward a common purpose. They also serve as mentors, coaches, and advocates for team members, helping them develop their skills and achieve their full potential.

Project Management: Project managers play a crucial position in making plans, organizing, and executing crew initiatives and responsibilities. They are answerable for defining project goals, creating timelines and milestones, allocating assets, and tracking progress toward dreams. Project managers also facilitate communication and collaboration among team members, resolve conflicts, and ensure that projects are completed on time and within budget.

Subject Matter Experts (SMEs): Subject professionals (SMEs) bring specialized understanding and knowledge to the team, regularly in specific areas such as generation, finance, advertising, or operations. They are responsible for providing insights, advice, and solutions related to their area of expertise, contributing to the overall success of the team's projects and initiatives.

Collaborators: Collaborators are adept at working closely with other team members to achieve shared goals. They are excellent communicators, active listeners, and relationship builders. Collaborators contribute ideas, feedback, and support, fostering an environment of trust and open dialogue that drives creativity and innovation.

Contributors: Contributors are crew individuals who excel at working closely with others to obtain shared desires. They are skilled communicators, active listeners, and adept at building relationships and fostering trust within the team. Contributors contribute ideas, feedback, and support to their teammates, helping to drive innovation and creativity.

Facilitators: Facilitators are team members who are skilled at organizing and leading group discussions, meetings, and workshops. They create supportive and inclusive surroundings in which all crew contributors feel comfortable sharing their thoughts and opinions. Facilitators also assist in preserving conferences on the course, controlling conflicts, and making certain that choices are made collaboratively and transparently.

Front Office Staff Roles

Front office staff play a crucial role in the smooth functioning of various organizations, particularly in industries such as hospitality, healthcare, retail, and professional services. Their responsibilities typically involve direct interaction with customers, clients, patients, or visitors. Here are some common roles and responsibilities of front office staff:

Receptionist: Receptionists are often the first point of contact for anyone entering an organization. Their responsibilities include greeting visitors, answering phone calls and emails, and directing inquiries to the appropriate person or department. They might also schedule appointments, manage calendars, and help with administrative obligations consisting of filing, fact-entering, and maintaining office resources.

Customer Service Representative: Customer service representatives interact directly with customers or clients to address inquiries, provide information, resolve complaints, and ensure a positive experience. They may handle a variety of tasks, including processing orders, handling returns or exchanges, and providing product or service recommendations. Customer service representatives must possess excellent communication skills, empathy, and problem-solving abilities.

Front Desk Clerk: Front desk clerks typically work in hospitality settings such as hotels, resorts, or airlines. Their responsibilities include checking guests in and out, processing reservations, handling payments, and providing information about hotel amenities, services, and local attractions. Front desk clerks also address guest concerns or requests and coordinate with other hotel staff to ensure guest satisfaction.

Administrative Assistant: Administrative assistants offer administrative assistance to executives, managers, or different staff contributors within a company. Their responsibilities may include managing calendars, scheduling meetings, preparing documents and reports, organizing files, and coordinating travel arrangements. Administrative assistants play a critical role in maintaining efficient workplace operations and helping the desires of the enterprise's group of workers.

Patient Services Representative: In healthcare settings, patient services representatives assist patients with appointment scheduling, registration, insurance verification, and billing inquiries. They may also collect patient information, update medical records, and coordinate referrals to specialists or other healthcare providers. Patient services representatives must maintain patient confidentiality and adhere to healthcare regulations.

Sales Associate: In retail environments, sales associates assist customers with product selection, provide information about merchandise, process transactions, and handle customer inquiries or complaints. They may also help with stocking shelves, organizing displays, and maintaining store cleanliness. Sales associates play a critical role in driving sales and ensuring customer satisfaction.

Communication Channels with the Billing Department

Effective communication channels with the billing department are essential for resolving billing inquiries, clarifying charges, and ensuring accurate billing practices. Here are some common communication channels that individuals or organizations can use to connect with the billing department:

Phone: One of the most direct and immediate communication channels is via phone. Customers or clients can call the billing department's committed cellphone number to speak with a representative without delay. Phone calls allow for real-time interaction, enabling individuals to ask questions, seek clarification, and resolve issues promptly.

Email: Email provides a convenient and asynchronous communication channel for contacting the billing department. Customers or clients can send inquiries, requests, or documentation related to billing concerns via email. Email communication allows for detailed explanations, attachments, and a written record of correspondence, which can be helpful for documentation purposes.

Online Portals: Many organizations offer online portals or customer self-service platforms where individuals can access their billing information, make payments, and submit inquiries directly to the billing department. These portals often provide a secure and convenient way to communicate with the billing department while giving customers or clients control over their accounts.

Live Chat: Some organizations offer live chat support on their website or through mobile apps, allowing customers or clients to engage in real-time text-based conversations with billing representatives. Live chat is convenient for quick questions or inquiries and can often provide immediate assistance without the need for a phone call.

In-Person Visits: In some cases, individuals may prefer or need to visit the billing department in person to discuss billing matters face-to-face. This option is particularly relevant for local businesses or organizations with physical locations where customers or clients can speak with billing representatives directly.

Postal Mail: While less common in today's digital age, postal mail remains a viable communication channel for sending inquiries, documentation, or payments to the billing department. Some individuals may prefer to communicate via traditional mail, especially for formal inquiries or disputes.

Mobile Apps: Many organizations offer mobile apps that allow customers or clients to manage their accounts, including billing inquiries and payments, directly from their smartphones or tablets. Mobile apps provide a convenient and accessible communication channel for individuals on the go.

Collaborative Approach to Claims Follow-Up

A collaborative technique to claims follow-up involves leveraging the collective expertise, assets, and perspectives of numerous stakeholders to ensure timely and effective resolution of coverage claims. Rather than relying solely on individual efforts or departmental silos, a collaborative approach fosters communication, cooperation, and synergy among different parties involved in the claims process. Here's how a collaborative approach can enhance claims follow-up:

Cross-Functional Coordination: By involving representatives from different departments, such as claims processing, customer service, underwriting, and legal, a collaborative approach facilitates cross-functional coordination. This ensures that all relevant parties are aligned and working together toward common goals, such as resolving claims accurately and efficiently.

Shared Information and Insights: Collaboration allows for the sharing of important data, insights, and status updates on claims. This helps stakeholders stay informed, anticipate potential challenges, and develop strategies for proactive follow-up.

Problem-Solving and Innovation: Collaborative brainstorming and problem-solving sessions allow teams to develop creative solutions to complex claims issues. By pooling expertise, stakeholders can explore new approaches and strategies for resolving claims.

Customer-Centric Focus: A collaborative approach places a strong emphasis on customer satisfaction and experience. By involving customer service representatives and other frontline staff in claims follow-up efforts, organizations can ensure that the needs and concerns of policyholders are prioritized and addressed promptly. This customer-centric focus helps build trust, loyalty, and positive relationships with policyholders.

Continuous Improvement: Collaboration enables organizations to evaluate and improve their claims follow-up processes continuously. By soliciting feedback from stakeholders, analyzing performance metrics, and implementing lessons learned, organizations can identify opportunities for optimization and refinement to enhance the efficiency and effectiveness of claims follow-up over time.

Chapter Reflection and Implementation Notes

What New Insights Did I Gain?

(Use this space to reflect on key takeaways from this chapter.)

How Can I Apply These Principles in My Practice?

(Note actionable steps or ideas inspired by this chapter.)

Additional Notes

(Use the lines below for any further notes, ideas, or observations.)

CHAPTER 14
CLAIMS SUBMISSION BEST PRACTICES

Claims submission is a critical process in the insurance industry that requires attention to detail, accuracy, and adherence to best practices to ensure efficient processing and timely reimbursement. Here are some key best practices for claims submission.

Complete and Accurate Information

Ensure that all required fields in the claims form are filled out accurately and completely. This consists of presenting precise information about the incident or loss, relevant dates, policyholder records, and any supporting documentation or evidence.

Timely Submission

Submit the claim as soon as possible after the care of the patient or incident occurs. Delays in claims submission can lead to processing bottlenecks, extended wait times for reimbursement, and potential complications in claim resolution.

Follow Proper Procedures

Familiarize yourself with the specific claims submission procedures and requirements of your insurance provider. This may include using designated forms, submitting claims through preferred channels, and adhering to any specific documentation or formatting guidelines.

Document Retention

Keep copies of all relevant documentation and correspondence related to the claim, including claim forms, receipts, invoices, photos, and communication with the insurance company. This documentation serves as a record of the claim submission process and can be valuable for reference or documentation purposes.

Clear and Concise Communication

Provide clear and concise information in your claims submission, avoiding unnecessary details or ambiguity. Clearly articulate the nature of the condition, the extent of care provided or injuries, and any relevant circumstances or factors that may impact the claim.

Review and Verification

Before submitting the claim, review the information carefully to ensure accuracy and consistency. Double-check important details such as policy numbers, claim amounts, diagnosis coding, Current Procedural Terminology (CPT), Healthcare Procedure Coding System (HCPCS), and contact information to avoid errors or discrepancies that could delay processing.

Follow-Up on Claims

After filing the claim, follow up with the insurance business enterprise to verify receipt and inquire about the status of the claim. Proactive communication expedites processing and ensures that any additional records or documentation required is supplied promptly.

Accuracy in Patient Information Collection

Accuracy in patient information collection is paramount in the healthcare industry to ensure patient safety, provide quality care, and maintain regulatory compliance. Here are key reasons why accuracy in patient information collection is essential:

Patient Safety

Accurate patient records are crucial for healthcare providers to make informed decisions about diagnosis, treatment, and medication management. Errors or inaccuracies in patient information, such as incorrect medical history or allergies, can jeopardize patient safety.

Quality of Care

Healthcare providers rely on accurate patient information to deliver high-quality care tailored to each patient's unique needs and medical history. Accurate information enables providers to develop comprehensive care plans, monitor progress effectively, and identify potential health risks or complications.

Continuity of Care

Accurate patient statistics facilitate seamless communication and coordination of care among healthcare providers across different settings, such as hospitals, clinics, and primary care offices. This continuity of care ensures that patients receive consistent, complete care and reduces the risk of fragmented or duplicated services.

Legal and Regulatory Compliance

Healthcare organizations are subject to strict regulatory requirements and standards related to patient information privacy, security, and accuracy. Ensuring accuracy in patient records collection allows healthcare companies to follow legal guidelines such as the Health Insurance Portability and Accountability Act (HIPAA) and preserve patient confidentiality and privacy rights.

Billing and Reimbursement

Accurate patient information is essential for accurate billing and reimbursement processes. Errors or discrepancies in patient demographic information, insurance coverage, or treatment codes can result in claim denials, delayed payments, or billing disputes, impacting the financial health of healthcare organizations and patients alike.

Timely Submission of Claims

Timely submission of claims is crucial in the insurance industry to ensure prompt processing, expedite reimbursement, and maintain regulatory compliance. Here are key reasons why timely submission of claims is essential:

Maximizing Reimbursement

Submitting claims promptly after the visit or incident increases the likelihood of receiving timely reimbursement from the insurance company. Delays in claims submission can result in processing bottlenecks, extended wait times for reimbursement, and potential cash flow issues for the policyholders or healthcare providers.

Preventing Claim Denials

Many insurance policies have specific deadlines or timeframes for submitting claims after a healthcare event occurs. Failure to submit claims within these deadlines can lead to claim denials or reduced reimbursement amounts, as insurers may deem the claim untimely and ineligible for coverage.

Ensuring Accuracy

Timely submission of claims allows for more accurate documentation of the medical occurrence or incident, reducing the likelihood of errors, discrepancies, or missing information in the claims process. Accurate and comprehensive claims documentation is essential for expedited processing and successful resolution of claims.

Compliance with Regulations

In many industries, such as healthcare and workers' compensation, there are regulatory requirements and deadlines for submitting claims to insurance carriers or government agencies. Timely submission of claims ensures compliance with these regulations and avoids potential penalties or fines for noncompliance.

Customer Satisfaction

Timely processing of claims is critical for maintaining positive relationships with policyholders, patients, or clients. Prompt reimbursement and resolution of claims demonstrate the insurance company's commitment to customer service, responsiveness, and reliability, enhancing overall satisfaction and loyalty.

Electronic Submission Platforms

Electronic submission platforms have revolutionized the way claims are processed in various industries, providing efficient, secure, and streamlined methods for submitting, processing, and managing claims electronically. These platforms offer numerous benefits for insurance companies, healthcare providers, and other organizations involved in claims processing. Here are some key advantages of electronic submission platforms:

Benefits of Electronic Submission Platforms

Efficiency: Electronic submission platforms eliminate the need for manual paper-based processes, saving time and resources for both the submitting party and the recipient. Claims can be submitted electronically in a matter of minutes, reducing processing times and accelerating reimbursement.

Accuracy: Electronic submission platforms help minimize errors and inaccuracies commonly associated with manual data entry. Built-in validation checks and error correction features ensure that claims are complete, accurate, and compliant with regulatory requirements, reducing the likelihood of claim denials or rejections.

Cost Savings: By transitioning from paper-based processes to digital submission systems, organizations can significantly reduce administrative costs associated with printing, mailing, and storing paper documents. Electronic submissions also eliminate the need for postage, envelopes, and other mailing supplies, further reducing operational expenses.

Accessibility: Electronic submission platforms provide convenient access to claims submission and processing capabilities anytime and anywhere. Users can submit claims online from any internet-enabled device, making it easier to manage claims remotely or on the go.

Security: Electronic submission platforms incorporate advanced security features such as encryption, user authentication, and audit reporting to protect sensitive patient or customer information. These platforms comply with industry standards and regulations such as HIPAA in healthcare, ensuring the confidentiality, integrity, and privacy of electronic claims data.

Integration: Many electronic submission platforms seamlessly integrate with existing practice management systems, electronic health records (EHR), or insurance systems, allowing for seamless data exchange and interoperability. Integration streamlines workflows, reduces duplication of efforts, and enhances data accuracy and consistency across systems.

Chapter Reflection and Implementation Notes

What New Insights Did I Gain?

(Use this space to reflect on key takeaways from this chapter.)

How Can I Apply These Principles in My Practice?

(Note actionable steps or ideas inspired by this chapter.)

Additional Notes

(Use the lines below for any further notes, ideas, or observations.)

CHAPTER 15
CLAIMS TRACKING SYSTEM

A claims tracking system is a vital tool used by insurance companies, healthcare providers, and other organizations to monitor and manage the entire lifecycle of insurance claims from submission to resolution. This system provides a centralized platform for monitoring, organizing, and processing claims efficiently. Here are some key features and benefits of a claims tracking system:

Key Features and Benefits of a Claims Tracking System

Centralized Repository: A claims tracking system acts as a centralized database where all claims-related documents, correspondence, forms, and payment records are stored. This centralized system ensures that all the necessary data is accessible and well organized, allowing users to retrieve essential information quickly.

Real-Time Updates: The system provides real-time tracking of claims, offering visibility into every stage of the claim lifecycle. This includes submission, processing, approval, or denial. Users receive notifications of important milestones, such as when a claim requires further documentation or when payment is due.

Workflow Automation: Automation is key to increasing the speed and accuracy of claims processing. A claims tracking system automates repetitive tasks such as claim routing, assigning follow-up tasks, sending reminders, and updating status changes. By automating these tasks, organizations reduce human error and improve overall productivity.

Customizable Dashboards and Reports: Claims tracking systems allow users to create personalized dashboards that display key performance indicators (KPIs), trends, and detailed reports. These reports can track metrics like claim approval rates, processing times, and reimbursement amounts, helping organizations identify areas of improvement.

Integration Capabilities: Claims tracking systems can be integrated with other healthcare or business software, such as practice management systems, electronic health records (EHR), and billing software. This seamless integration facilitates data sharing across departments and enhances coordination between teams, reducing duplication and improving efficiency.

Compliance and Audit Reporting: Claims tracking systems generate detailed audit reports that log every action taken on a claim, including who accessed it, what changes were made, and when those changes occurred. This feature supports regulatory compliance by ensuring accountability and transparency in the claims process.

Enhanced Customer Service: The transparency provided by claims tracking systems improves communication with patients, policyholders, and clients. The ability to share real-time status updates on claims ensures that customers are informed and satisfied with the progress, leading to increased trust and better relationships with stakeholders.

Introduction to Claims Tracking Software

One of the most important activities in the insurance industry is claims processing. Years ago, the process was entirely manual, slow, and paper based, with no role for IT. The complexity of managing claims and the hand-operated process led to irreversible errors and delays, which severely harmed customer relationships.

However, automation technology has provided some relief. Programmed software streamlined processes and improved claim accuracy. As a result, it is appropriate to introduce claims management software as a powerful tool that ensures claims are processed efficiently and successfully.

The advancement of new technology in the insurance landscape improved things. Insurance claims management software revitalized the entire claim cycle, making it faster and less prone to errors. Insurance companies use the software to manage and evaluate claims. It enables agents to manage the claims process through automated workflows, ensuring that all claim details are stored in a centralized system. The claims processing software facilitates the entire process, from claim creation to calculation, payment, and closure.

It automates the process, shortens processing time, reduces costs, and thus improves the customer experience throughout the claims process. It even reduces the likelihood of fraud while increasing efficiency. The claims management system accelerates the process, resulting in faster outcomes for both the customer and the insurance provider.

Claims tracking software is a vital tool for organizations that process insurance claims. Over the years, claims processing was traditionally manual and prone to errors, leading to delays and customer dissatisfaction. The introduction of claims tracking software revolutionized the process by automating various tasks, speeding up claims submission and adjudication, and providing greater accuracy.

Benefits of Claims Tracking Software

- **Automation:** The software automates the entire claim cycle, from creation to payment, reducing processing time and minimizing manual errors.
- **Cost Efficiency:** By streamlining workflows and reducing administrative costs associated with manual processes, claims tracking software offers significant cost savings for organizations.
- **Improved Accuracy:** Automated workflows and validation checks ensure that claims are processed with a high degree of accuracy, reducing the risk of claim denials or rejections due to errors.

Implementation and Training

Implementation and training are crucial aspects of adopting any new software system, including claims tracking software. A well-planned implementation strategy and comprehensive training program are essential to ensure successful adoption, user proficiency, and maximum utilization of the software's capabilities. Here's a closer look at implementation and training for claims tracking software:

Needs Assessment: It's essential to conduct a thorough needs assessment to understand the specific requirements, workflows, and challenges of the organization. This assessment helps identify key stakeholders, define objectives, and tailor the implementation plan to meet the organization's unique needs.

Project Planning: Develop a detailed project plan that outlines the timeline, milestones, and responsibilities for implementing the claims tracking software. Assign roles and duties to team members, establish communication channels, and set clear expectations for the implementation process.

Software Configuration: Work closely with the software vendor or implementation team to configure the claims tracking software according to the organization's requirements. This may include setting up user accounts, customizing workflows, and integrating the software with other systems or applications.

User Training: Provide comprehensive training to users on how to use the claims tracking software effectively. Training sessions should cover basic navigation, functionality, and best practices for claims management. Offer hands-on exercises, demonstrations, and user guides to support learning and skill development.

Ongoing Support: Offer continuous guidance and support to users as they begin using the claims tracking software in their daily operations. Provide access to support resources, such as online tutorials, knowledge bases, and user forums, and designate a support team to address technical issues or user questions.

Feedback and Evaluation: Solicit feedback from users throughout the implementation process to identify areas for improvement and address any concerns or challenges. Conduct regular evaluations to assess user satisfaction, software performance, and alignment with organizational goals, and adjust as needed.

Monitoring and Reporting

Monitoring and reporting are essential features of a claims tracking system that allow organizations to measure the effectiveness of their claims management processes. With real-time data, customizable dashboards, and performance reports, users can easily track claims activity and identify trends or issues.

Key Aspects of Monitoring and Reporting

Real-Time Monitoring: Real-time updates allow users to see the current status of each claim, track pending tasks, and ensure that deadlines are met. This helps users stay on top of claims and take prompt action when issues arise.

Claims Performance Reports: Generate reports that analyze various aspects of claims processing, such as claim approval rates, the frequency of denials, and average processing times. These insights help organizations identify bottlenecks, inefficiencies, and areas for improvement.

KPI Tracking: Claims tracking systems allow organizations to define and track key performance indicators (KPIs) related to claims processing. This includes metrics such as:

- Claims submitted per day
- Average time to process a claim
- Denial rates
- Average reimbursement amounts

Audit Reporting: Monitoring audit reports provides a comprehensive record of all actions taken on a claim. This is critical for maintaining compliance with regulatory standards and provides transparency in case of disputes or reviews.

Chapter Reflection and Implementation Notes

What New Insights Did I Gain?

(Use this space to reflect on key takeaways from this chapter.)

How Can I Apply These Principles in My Practice?

(Note actionable steps or ideas inspired by this chapter.)

Additional Notes

(Use the lines below for any further notes, ideas, or observations.)

CHAPTER 16
IDENTIFYING AND ADDRESSING DENIALS

Denials occur when an insurance company determines that a claim does not meet the criteria for coverage or reimbursement under the policy. Here's how organizations can effectively identify and address denials.

Claims Scrubbing

Implement a claims scrubbing process to review claims for errors or inconsistencies before submission. This involves conducting thorough reviews of claims data, coding accuracy, and compliance with billing regulations to minimize the risk of denials due to preventable errors.

Automated Denial Management Systems

Utilize automated denial management systems to streamline the identification and resolution of denials. These systems analyze claim data, identify patterns or trends in denials, and generate reports to help prioritize and address denials efficiently. Automated workflows and alerts can also facilitate timely follow-up and resolution of denied claims.

Root Cause Analysis

Conduct root cause analysis to identify the underlying reasons for denials and address systemic issues contributing to recurring denials. This involves analyzing denial trends, identifying common reasons for denials, and implementing corrective actions to prevent future occurrences.

Appeals Process

Develop a structured appeals process to challenge denied claims and advocate for reimbursement on behalf of the policyholder or patient. This may involve gathering additional documentation or evidence to support the claim, preparing appeals letters or forms, and engaging in direct communication with the insurance company to resolve disputes.

Provider Education and Training

Provide ongoing education and training to healthcare providers, billing staff, and other stakeholders involved in claims submission to improve awareness of billing regulations, coding guidelines, and documentation requirements. Enhanced knowledge and skills can help reduce errors and minimize the likelihood of denials.

Continuous Monitoring and Improvement

Continuously monitor denial rates, track performance metrics, and evaluate the effectiveness of denial management strategies. Regularly review denial data, assess the impact of interventions, and make adjustments as needed to optimize claims management processes and reduce denials over time.

Analyzing Denial Reasons

Here's how organizations can effectively analyze denial reasons:

First, categorize denial reasons into distinct categories, such as coding errors, documentation deficiencies, eligibility issues, and contractual discrepancies. This helps in organizing and prioritizing analysis efforts.

Next, utilize data analytics tools and software to analyze denial trends and patterns across various dimensions such as payer, provider, service type, and denial code. These tools help identify common trends and root causes contributing to denials.

Conduct root cause analysis to investigate the underlying reasons for denials. This involves examining claims data, reviewing documentation, and engaging with stakeholders to identify systemic issues and process gaps contributing to denials.

Developing Strategies for Common Denials

Developing strategies for common denials is essential for improving claims management efficiency and maximizing reimbursement rates.

Here's how organizations can develop effective strategies to address common denials:

Identify Common Denial Patterns: Analyze denial data to identify recurring denial reasons and patterns. Categorize denials into common themes such as coding errors, documentation deficiencies, eligibility issues, or authorization requirements.

Root Cause Analysis: Conduct root cause analysis to understand the underlying reasons for common denials. Determine whether denials stem from systemic issues, process gaps, or individual errors. This analysis helps in developing targeted strategies to address the root causes of denials.

Provider Education and Training: Provide education and training to healthcare providers, billing staff, and other stakeholders to improve awareness of common denial reasons and billing regulations. Training programs should focus on coding accuracy, documentation requirements, and proper claims submission practices.

Enhancing Documentation: Implement standard documentation templates and workflows to ensure that medical records adequately support the services provided. Provide guidance to providers on documenting services, procedures, and medical necessity to support claims submissions.

Streamlining Authorization Processes: Develop a structured appeals process to challenge denied claims and advocate for reimbursement. Establish clear guidelines for appealing denials, gathering additional documentation, and communicating with payers effectively to resolve disputes.

Continuous Monitoring and Improvement: Continuously monitor denial rates, track performance metrics, and evaluate the effectiveness of denial management strategies.

Resubmission Procedures and Guidelines

Resubmission procedures and guidelines are essential components of the claims management process, enabling organizations to address denied claims and advocate for reimbursement effectively. Here's how organizations can establish resubmission procedures and guidelines:

Review Denial Reasons: Before resubmitting a denied claim, carefully review the denial reason provided by the payer.

Understand why the claim was denied and identify any necessary actions or documentation required for resubmission.

Correct Errors: If the denial was due to errors or inaccuracies in the original claim submission, correct these errors before resubmitting the claim. This may involve updating coding information, providing additional documentation, or correcting billing discrepancies.

Provide Additional Documentation: If the denial requires additional information or documentation to support the claim, gather this information promptly. Ensure that all required documentation is complete, accurate, and compliant with payer requirements before resubmitting the claim.

Follow Payer Guidelines: Adhere to payer-specific resubmission guidelines and requirements when preparing the claim for resubmission. Pay attention to any deadlines, formatting preferences, or documentation requirements specified by the payer to avoid further delays or denials.

Document Resubmission Efforts: Keep detailed records of all resubmission efforts, including communications with the payer, documentation provided, and any follow-up actions taken. This documentation serves as a record of your efforts to resolve the denial and may be useful if further appeals are necessary.

Track Resubmission Status: Monitor the status of resubmitted claims closely to ensure timely processing and resolution. Follow up with the payer if necessary to confirm receipt of the resubmitted claim and inquire about the status of processing.

Chapter Reflection and Implementation Notes

What New Insights Did I Gain?

(Use this space to reflect on key takeaways from this chapter.)

How Can I Apply These Principles in My Practice?

(Note actionable steps or ideas inspired by this chapter.)

Additional Notes

(Use the lines below for any further notes, ideas, or observations.)

CHAPTER 17
EFFECTIVE COMMUNICATION WITH PAYERS

Effective communication with payers is essential for successful claims management and reimbursement. Here are key strategies for maintaining effective communication with payers:

Clear and Concise Communication: Ensure that all communications with payers are clear, concise, and professional. Clearly state the purpose of the communication, provide relevant details, and avoid unnecessary jargon or technical language.

Timely Follow-Up: Follow up promptly on submitted claims to inquire about the status of processing or to address any issues or concerns. Timely follow-up demonstrates proactive communication and helps expedite the resolution of claims.

Utilize Preferred Communication Channels: Payers may have preferred communication channels for inquiries, appeals, or other correspondence. Use these channels whenever possible to ensure that communications are received and processed efficiently.

Provide Complete Documentation: When submitting claims or responding to payer inquiries, provide complete and accurate documentation to support the claim. Include all necessary information, such as medical records, treatment plans, and billing codes, to facilitate timely processing and reimbursement.

Maintain Professionalism: In all correspondence with payers, maintain a professional manner, even in cases of disputes or disagreements. Approach communication with a collaborative mindset, seeking to resolve issues amicably and to maintain positive relationships with payers.

Document Communication: Keep detailed records of all verbal exchanges with payers, including phone calls, emails, and written correspondence. Document the date, time, nature of the communication, and any follow-up actions taken to ensure accountability and to facilitate tracking of resolution efforts.

Establishing Clear Lines of Communication

An organization's ability to collaborate and coordinate effectively depends on the establishment of clear channels of communication. Here's how organizations can establish clear lines of communication:

Define Roles and Responsibilities: Establish explicit guidelines for the duties and responsibilities of the organization's departments, stakeholders, and team members. Ensure that everyone understands their responsibilities and how they contribute to overall goals and objectives.

Establish Communication Channels: Identify and establish suitable communication channels for different types of communication, such as email, phone, video conferencing, and project management platforms. Use these channels consistently to facilitate efficient communication and information sharing.

Set Expectations: Clearly communicate expectations for communication frequency, responsiveness, and etiquette within the organization. Establish guidelines for responding to emails, returning phone calls, and attending meetings to ensure timely and effective communication.

Encourage Open Communication: Foster an environment of open communication where team members feel comfortable sharing thoughts, concerns, and feedback. Encourage active listening, respectful dialogue, and constructive criticism to facilitate meaningful communication and collaboration.

Provide Training and Support: Offer training and support to team members on effective communication techniques, tools, and technologies. Provide resources such as communication templates, guidelines, and best practices to support effective communication practices.

Regular Check-Ins: Hold regular check-in meetings to ensure alignment and to address any communication challenges that arise. These meetings help maintain consistency, build rapport, and reinforce accountability among team members.

Professional Correspondence, Follow-Up Calls, and Inquiries: Best Practices

Professional correspondence is essential for maintaining strong relationships, conveying information effectively, and representing the organization positively.

Use Proper Salutations and Sign-Offs: Begin correspondence with a respectful salutation, such as "Dear [Name]" or "Hello [Title] [Last Name]," and end with a professional sign-off, such as "Sincerely," "Best regards," or "Thank you."

Be Clear and Concise: Use straightforward language to convey your message. Keep correspondence concise and focused, avoiding unnecessary details or verbosity.

Use a Professional Tone and Language: Maintain a professional tone throughout, avoiding slang, abbreviations, or informal language. Use courteous language and avoid excessive punctuation or all capital letters, which may come across as aggressive or unprofessional.

Proofread Before Sending: Always proofread correspondence before sending it. Check for spelling, grammar, and punctuation errors, as typos or mistakes can detract from professionalism and credibility.

Personalize When Appropriate: Personalize correspondence when appropriate by addressing the recipient by name and referencing relevant information or previous interactions. This demonstrates attentiveness and helps foster a stronger connection.

Respond Promptly: Respond to correspondence promptly, ideally within 24–48 hours. Even if you need more time to provide a thorough response, acknowledge receipt of the message and provide an estimated timeline for follow-up.

Follow Company Guidelines: Adhere to any company or organizational guidelines for correspondence, including formatting, branding, and confidentiality policies.

Chapter Reflection and Implementation Notes

What New Insights Did I Gain?

(Use this space to reflect on key takeaways from this chapter.)

How Can I Apply These Principles in My Practice?

(Note actionable steps or ideas inspired by this chapter.)

Additional Notes

(Use the lines below for any further notes, ideas, or observations.)

CHAPTER 18
MONITORING OUTSTANDING CLAIMS

Monitoring outstanding claims is essential for effective claims management and reimbursement. Here are key steps for monitoring outstanding claims:

Establish a Tracking System: Implement a tracking system to monitor the status of outstanding claims. This system should include relevant details such as claim number, date of submission, payer information, and current status.

Regular Reviews: Conduct regular reviews of outstanding claims to identify trends, patterns, and areas for improvement. Review aging reports and prioritize follow-up efforts based on the age and value of outstanding claims.

Follow-Up Procedures: Develop standardized procedures for follow-up on outstanding claims. Determine appropriate timelines for follow-up based on payer requirements and industry standards. Assign responsibility for follow-up tasks to specific staff members or departments.

Utilize Technology: Leverage technology solutions such as claims management software or electronic health record (EHR) systems to streamline monitoring and follow-up on outstanding claims. These systems can automate tasks, generate reports, and provide real-time updates on claim status.

Communication with Payers: Maintain open lines of communication with payers to inquire about the status of outstanding claims, resolve any issues or discrepancies, and advocate for timely reimbursement.

Documentation: Maintain detailed records of all communications and follow-up efforts related to pending claims. Document the date, time, nature of the communication, and any actions taken to facilitate tracking and accountability.

Regular Audits and Reviews

Regular audits and reviews are essential components of quality assurance and compliance in various industries, including healthcare, finance, and manufacturing. Here are key reasons why regular audits and reviews are important:

Identifying Errors and Inconsistencies: Regular audits and reviews help identify errors, inconsistencies, and deviations from established standards or procedures. By conducting thorough reviews of processes, documentation, and data, organizations can detect and correct issues before they escalate.

Ensuring Compliance: Audits and reviews ensure compliance with regulatory requirements, industry standards, and internal policies. Regular audits help organizations identify areas of non-compliance and take corrective action to mitigate risks and avoid penalties.

Improving Efficiency: Audits and reviews identify inefficiencies, bottlenecks, and areas for improvement in business processes. By analyzing performance metrics and identifying opportunities for optimization, organizations can streamline operations, reduce costs, and improve overall efficiency.

Enhancing Quality: Regular audits and reviews contribute to ongoing quality improvement efforts. By evaluating products or services, customer feedback, and overall performance metrics, businesses can identify opportunities for improvement and provide enhanced products or services to clients.

Mitigating Risks: Audits and reviews help organizations identify and mitigate risks related to fraud, errors, data breaches, and other potential threats. By proactively identifying risks and implementing controls and safeguards, organizations can minimize the likelihood and impact of adverse events.

Promoting Accountability and Transparency: Regular audits promote accountability and transparency within organizations. By conducting independent assessments of processes and controls, organizations demonstrate their commitment to integrity, accountability, and ethical behavior.

Addressing Aging Claims

Aging claims refer to claims that have been outstanding for an extended period and have yet to be processed or paid by the payer within the expected timeframe. Here are key steps for addressing aging claims:

Identify Aging Claims: Review aging reports regularly to identify claims that have been outstanding beyond the expected timeframe. Categorize aging claims based on the length of time outstanding and prioritize follow-up efforts accordingly.

Conduct Follow-Up: Initiate follow-up procedures for aging claims, including contacting the payer to inquire about the status of the claim, identifying reasons for delays, and advocating for timely resolution.

Escalate as Needed: If aging claims remain unresolved after initial follow-up efforts, escalate the issue to higher levels of management or engage with payer representatives to address concerns and expedite resolution.

Document Communication: Maintain detailed records of all communications and follow-up efforts related to aging claims. Document the date, time, nature of the communication, and any actions taken to facilitate tracking and accountability.

Utilize Technology: Leverage technology solutions such as claims management software or EHR systems to streamline monitoring and follow-up on aging claims. These systems can automate tasks, generate reports, and provide real-time updates on claim status.

Setting Performance Metrics

Here are key steps for setting performance metrics:

Define Objectives: Clearly define the overarching objectives or goals that you want to achieve. These objectives should be specific, measurable, achievable, relevant, and time-bound (SMART).

Identify Key Performance Indicators (KPIs): Determine the key areas or aspects of performance that align with your objectives. KPIs should be quantifiable metrics that can be used to measure progress and success.

Consider Stakeholder Input: Involve stakeholders, including employees, managers, and customers, in the process of identifying relevant KPIs. Consider their input and perspectives to ensure that the selected metrics are meaningful and reflective of organizational priorities.

Set Targets: Establish targets or benchmarks for each KPI based on historical performance, industry standards, or organizational goals. Targets should be challenging yet achievable and should provide a clear indication of success.

Monitor and Evaluate: Regularly monitor performance against established metrics and targets. Use data analytics tools and reporting systems to track progress, identify trends, and analyze performance data.

Adjust as Needed: Continuously evaluate the relevance and effectiveness of performance metrics. Adjust metrics or targets as needed based on changes in organizational priorities, market conditions, or stakeholder feedback.

Chapter Reflection and Implementation Notes

What New Insights Did I Gain?

(Use this space to reflect on key takeaways from this chapter.)

How Can I Apply These Principles in My Practice?

(Note actionable steps or ideas inspired by this chapter.)

Additional Notes

(Use the lines below for any further notes, ideas, or observations.)

CHAPTER 19
CONTINUOUS STAFF TRAINING AND DEVELOPMENT

Continuous staff training and development are essential for fostering a skilled, motivated, and adaptable workforce. Here are key benefits and strategies for implementing continuous staff training and development:

Skill Enhancement: Regular training programs help employees acquire new abilities, expand their expertise base, and stay up to date on industry trends and best practices. This enables them to perform their job roles more effectively and contribute to organizational success.

Employee Engagement: Investing in education and development demonstrates a dedication to employee growth and development, which can enhance job satisfaction, morale, and engagement. Engaged personnel are much more likely to be efficient, dependable, and invested in the achievement of the business or organization.

Retention and Recruitment: Offering opportunities for growth and advancement through training and development programs can improve employee retention rates and attract top talent. Employees are much more likely to stay with an enterprise that invests in their professional improvement and provides opportunities for career development.

Adaptability and Innovation: Continuous education and improvement assist personnel in adapting to adjustments in technology, processes, and marketplace dynamics. It fosters a tradition of innovation, agility, and continuous improvement, enabling corporations to stay competitive and be responsive to evolving enterprise needs.

Leadership Development: Training and development programs can identify and cultivate future leaders within the organization. Leadership development initiatives help employees develop critical leadership skills, build confidence, and prepare for leadership roles.

Feedback and Evaluation: Regular feedback and evaluation mechanisms are essential to evaluate the effectiveness of training and development programs. Solicit feedback from participants to identify strengths, areas for improvement, and future training needs.

Keeping Staff Informed of Industry Changes

It's crucial to keep staff members updated about industry changes so they are aware of the newest practices, laws, and advancements in their areas. Here are some effective strategies for keeping staff informed of industry changes:

Regular Communication: Create regular communication channels to share updates, news, and industry trends with employees. This may include email newsletters, internal memos, or dedicated communication platforms.

Workshops and Seminars: Provide opportunities for staff to attend training sessions, workshops, webinars, or conferences related to their industry. These events offer valuable insights, networking opportunities, and exposure to emerging trends and best practices.

Knowledge-Sharing Sessions: Organize knowledge-sharing sessions where staff can exchange information, experiences, and insights about industry developments. To promote a culture of ongoing learning, team members should be encouraged to communicate freely and work together.

Utilize Online Resources: Curate a list of reputable online resources, blogs, industry publications, and websites that provide relevant information and updates about the industry. Encourage staff to explore these resources to stay informed regularly.

Assign Research Tasks: Assign research tasks or projects to staff members to investigate specific industry topics, trends, or developments. This encourages independent learning and empowers employees to take ownership of their professional development.

Update Training Materials: Ensure that training materials, manuals, and documentation are regularly updated to reflect changes in industry regulations, standards, or best practices. Provide access to updated resources and encourage staff to refer to them as needed.

Feedback Mechanisms: Encourage staff to provide feedback on industry changes, training programs, and communication efforts. Solicit suggestions for improvement and adjust strategies as needed to better meet the needs of employees.

Ongoing Training on Claims Processes

Ongoing training on claims processes is essential for ensuring that staff members possess the knowledge, skills, and expertise required to manage claims effectively and optimize reimbursement. Here are key benefits and strategies for implementing ongoing training on claims processes:

Maintaining Compliance: Claims processes are subject to frequent changes in regulations, payer requirements, and industry standards. Staff personnel are kept up to date on pertinent laws, rules, and compliance standards by ongoing training, which helps them avoid mistakes and penalties.

Improving Efficiency: Continuous training helps staff members refine their understanding of claims processes, identify opportunities for streamlining workflows, and adopt best practices to improve efficiency and productivity.

Enhancing Accuracy: Training programs reinforce proper coding practices, documentation requirements, and claims submission protocols, leading to higher accuracy in claims processing. This reduces the likelihood of denials, rejections, and delays in reimbursement.

Addressing Emerging Trends: Employees can stay up to date on the latest innovations, technology, and trends in claims processing through ongoing training. This allows organizations to adapt to changes in the industry landscape and leverage new opportunities for development.

Promoting Professional Development: Training programs offer possibilities for staff members to acquire new skills, expand their knowledge base, and develop their careers within the organization. Investing in staff development fosters employee engagement, loyalty, and job satisfaction.

Feedback and Evaluation: Solicit feedback from the workforce to evaluate the effectiveness of training programs and identify areas for improvement. Regular evaluation ensures that training initiatives align with staff needs and organizational goals.

Encouraging Professional Growth

Encouraging professional growth among employees is essential for fostering a skilled, motivated, and engaged workforce. Here are key strategies for promoting professional growth within an organization:

Offering Diverse Learning Opportunities: Provide access to training programs, workshops, seminars, webinars, and conferences to support ongoing skill development and career advancement. Encourage employees to pursue certifications, further education, or specialized training relevant to their roles.

Create Individual Development Plans: Work with employees to create individual development plans that outline their career goals, areas for growth, and action steps for achieving professional advancement. Provide guidance, resources, and support to help employees reach their full potential.

Provide Mentorship and Coaching: Pair employees with experienced mentors or coaches who can offer guidance, feedback, and advice on professional development, skill enhancement, and overcoming challenges. Mentorship programs facilitate knowledge transfer, skill-building, and career progression.

Recognize and Reward Achievements: Recognize and celebrate employees' accomplishments, milestones, and contributions to the organization. Provide meaningful rewards, incentives, or opportunities for advancement to acknowledge and encourage professional growth. Celebrating achievements motivates employees to continue their professional development journey.

Encourage Continuous Learning: Foster a culture of continuous learning and self-improvement by providing opportunities for employees to explore new ideas, pursue interests outside of their immediate roles, and engage in lifelong learning. Support initiatives such as book clubs, lunch-and-learns, or online courses.

Promote Cross-Functional Exposure: Encourage employees to explore opportunities for cross-functional collaboration, job rotations, or project assignments that expose them to different roles, responsibilities, and perspectives within the organization. This broadens their skill set, expands their network, and fosters both personal and professional growth.

Escalation Protocols

An escalation protocol outlines the steps and procedures for handling issues or concerns that cannot be resolved through regular channels of communication or problem-solving. Here are the key components of an escalation protocol:

Definition of Escalation Criteria: Clearly define the criteria or circumstances that warrant escalation. This may include unresolved conflicts, significant delays, critical errors, or situations requiring urgent attention.

Chain of Command: Establish a hierarchical structure or chain of command outlining who to escalate issues to and in what order.

Identify specific individuals or roles responsible for addressing escalated issues at each level of the hierarchy.

Escalation Pathways: Define the specific pathways or channels through which issues should be escalated. This may include direct communication with supervisors, managers, department heads, or designated escalation contacts.

Escalation Triggers: Identify specific triggers or thresholds that prompt escalation, such as missed deadlines, repeated failures, or customer complaints. Establish clear criteria for determining when an issue should be escalated and to whom.

Timelines and Response Expectations: Establish timelines and response expectations for each stage of escalation. Define how quickly escalated issues should be addressed, communicated, and resolved to ensure timely resolution and prevent further escalation.

Documentation and Tracking: Implement systems for documenting and tracking escalated issues, including details of the problem, steps taken to address it, and outcomes. This ensures transparency, accountability, and continuity in managing escalated matters.

Reviewing and Refining Protocols: Periodically assess and evaluate the effectiveness of the escalation protocol. Identify areas for improvement, adjust procedures as needed, and provide training or guidance to staff on escalation procedures and protocols.

Handling Unresolved Issues

Handling unresolved issues effectively is essential for maintaining customer satisfaction, resolving conflicts, and preventing further escalation. Here are key steps for handling unresolved issues:

Acknowledging and Addressing Issues: Begin by acknowledging the customer's concerns and expressing empathy for their situation. Let them know that their feedback is valued and that you are committed to finding a resolution.

Gather Information: Listen actively to the customer's perspective and gather relevant information about the issue. Ask clarifying questions to fully understand the nature and scope of the problem.

Offer Solutions: Propose potential solutions or alternatives to address the customer's concerns. Be adaptable and willing to compromise, and customize your strategy to the unique requirements and preferences of the client.

Seek Assistance: Raise the problem to a manager, supervisor, or designated escalation contact if you are unable to handle it on your own. Provide them with a summary of the situation and any relevant background information.

Follow-Up: After escalating the issue, follow up with the customer to confirm that it is being addressed and provide updates on progress. Keep the customer informed throughout the resolution process to demonstrate transparency and accountability.

Learn and Improve: Take the opportunity to learn from unresolved issues and identify opportunities for improvement in products, services, or processes. Use feedback from unresolved issues to drive continuous improvement and prevent similar problems in the future.

Strategies for Continuous Improvement

Continuous improvement is essential for enhancing processes, products, and services over time. Key strategies for continuous improvement include:

Implementing the Kaizen Methodology: Use the Kaizen strategy, which promotes collaboration from all organizational levels and places emphasis on small, gradual adjustments to promote continuous development.

Data-Driven Decision-Making: Use statistical analytics and performance metrics to discover areas for improvement, measure development, and inform decision-making processes.

Feedback Loops: Establish feedback mechanisms to gather input from employees, customers, and stakeholders. Act on feedback to address concerns, identify opportunities, and drive improvement.

Lean Principles: Apply lean principles such as waste reduction, value stream mapping, and standardized work processes to streamline operations and improve efficiency.

Cross-Functional Collaboration: Foster collaboration and communication across departments and teams to leverage diverse perspectives and expertise in problem-solving and innovation.

Training and Development: To develop the abilities, knowledge, and skills necessary to support efforts for continuous improvement, invest in staff training and development. Promote improvement initiatives.

Chapter Reflection and Implementation Notes

What New Insights Did I Gain?

(Use this space to reflect on key takeaways from this chapter.)

How Can I Apply These Principles in My Practice?

(Note actionable steps or ideas inspired by this chapter.)

Additional Notes

(Use the lines below for any further notes, ideas, or observations.)

CONCLUSION

Effective management of claims processes is essential for ensuring operational efficiency, maximizing revenue, and maintaining customer satisfaction in various industries. From understanding the claims lifecycle to implementing continuous improvement strategies, organizations can streamline operations and optimize reimbursement by employing a combination of best practices, training, and communication protocols.

By establishing clear lines of communication, encouraging professional growth, and implementing escalation protocols, organizations can address challenges proactively and resolve issues efficiently. Additionally, ongoing training on claims processes and continuous improvement strategies enable organizations to adapt to changes in regulations, technology, and market dynamics, driving operational excellence and long-term success.

Recap of Key Points

- **Understanding the Claims Process:** Familiarize with the claims lifecycle, including submission, adjudication, and denials.
- **Importance of Effective Claims Follow-Up:** Emphasize the significance of timely follow-up to ensure reimbursement and resolve issues promptly.
- **Common Reasons for Claims Denials:** Highlight typical causes of claims denials, such as coding errors, lack of documentation, and eligibility issues.

- **Team Roles and Responsibilities:** Define roles within the team, including front office staff responsible for initial claim submission and follow-up.
- **Collaborative Approach to Claims Follow-Up:** Stress the importance of teamwork and communication channels between departments, especially with the billing department.
- **Claims Submission Best Practices:** Outline best practices for accurate and timely claims submission to minimize denials and delays.
- **Accuracy in Patient Information Collection:** Emphasize the importance of precise patient information collection to avoid billing errors and denials.
- **Timely Submission of Claims:** Stress the significance of submitting claims promptly to expedite reimbursement and prevent delays.
- **Electronic Submission Platforms:** Highlight the benefits of electronic submission platforms for efficient claims processing and tracking.
- **Claims Tracking System:** Introduce claims tracking software for monitoring claim status, identifying bottlenecks, and facilitating follow-up.
- **Identifying and Addressing Denials:** Discuss strategies for identifying denial reasons and implementing effective resolution procedures.
- **Professional Correspondence/Tips:** Provide guidelines for writing professional correspondence with payers and other stakeholders.

Reinforcing the Importance of Claims Follow-Up

Emphasizing the importance of claims follow-up is crucial for ensuring timely reimbursement and minimizing revenue loss for healthcare providers and insurance companies. Here are some key points to reinforce this importance:

- **Maximizing Revenue:** Effective follow-up ensures that claims are processed promptly and accurately, leading to quicker reimbursement and improved cash flow for the organization.

- **Reducing Denials:** Timely follow-up allows for the identification and resolution of issues that may lead to claim denials. Addressing these issues promptly helps minimize the risk of revenue loss due to denied claims.

- **Enhancing Patient Satisfaction:** Prompt resolution of claims leads to faster processing of insurance claims and reduces the likelihood of patients receiving unexpected bills or being billed incorrectly, thereby improving patient satisfaction.

- **Maintaining Financial Health:** Consistent follow-up on claims ensures that outstanding accounts receivable are actively managed, reducing the risk of aging claims and write-offs, which can negatively impact the organization's financial health.

- **Compliance and Accountability:** Demonstrating diligence in follow-up on claims reflects positively on the organization's commitment to compliance with payer requirements and accountability in revenue cycle management processes.

Case Reflection

Patient/Case:

Diagnosis/Treatment Approach:

Follow-Up or Insights:

CHAPTER 20: Conclusion

www.ingramcontent.com/pod-product-compliance
Lightning Source LLC
Chambersburg PA
CBHW050237270326
41914CB00034BA/1952/J

* 9 7 9 8 2 1 8 5 4 2 7 6 4 *